*May Sarton, Revisited*

Twayne's United States Authors Series

Warren French, Editor

*University of Wales, Swansea*

TUSAS 551

May Sarton. *Photograph* © *1986 Stathis Orphanos.*

*May Sarton, Revisited*

By Elizabeth Evans

*Georgia Institute of Technology*

*Twayne Publishers*
*A Division of G. K. Hall & Co.* • *Boston*

*May Sarton, Revisited*
Elizabeth Evans

Copyright 1989 by G. K. Hall & Co.
All rights reserved.
Published by Twayne Publishers
A Division of G. K. Hall & Co.
70 Lincoln Street
Boston, Massachusetts 02111

Copyediting supervised by Barbara Sutton
Book production by Janet Z. Reynolds
Book design by Barbara Anderson

Typeset in 11 pt. Garamond
by Compset, Inc., Beverly, Massachusetts

Printed on permanent/durable acid-free paper
and bound in the United States of America

**Library of Congress Cataloging-in-Publication Data**
Evans, Elizabeth, 1935-
    May Sarton, Revisited / by Elizabeth Evans.
        p.      cm. — (Twayne's United States authors series ; TUSAS 551)
    Bibliography: p.
    Includes index.
    ISBN 0-8057-7542-0 (alk. paper)
    1. Sarton, May, 1912–    —Criticism and interpretation.
I.   Title.   II.   Series.
PS3537.A832Z66    1989
811'.52—dc19                                                                89-30751
                                                                                     CIP

There is a continuum
(Those garlands of joined dancers)
Of redemptive love.

—May Sarton


*for family, friends*
*Joe, Carole, Ted*

# Contents

# Publisher's Note

*May Sarton, Revisited* by Elizabeth Evans is a timely retrospective of Sarton's literary career, and takes account of the numerous important works written by Sarton since 1973, when Twayne Publishers issued *May Sarton* by Agnes Sibley. We are pleased to offer this new evaluation of Sarton's lifetime achievement.

# About the Author

Elizabeth Evans received her Ph.D. in English from the University of North Carolina at Chapel Hill. Her publications include *Ring Lardner* (1979), *Eudora Welty* (1981), and *Thomas Wolfe* (1984) as well as articles on Welty, Wolfe, Edith Wharton, Doris Betts, and the nineteenth-century essayist and diplomat Alexander Hill Everett. Since 1964 Evans has taught English at the Georgia Institute of Technology.

# Preface

For over fifty years May Sarton has pursued her career as a writer and that process has been, as she says, "a long hard struggle." Above all, Sarton speaks for women, insisting that women claim their own identity, have their own lives. Sarton has been a model of the woman living alone, living a rich and full life. Without denying the dark side of solitude, she shows that the solitary life is not a deprived life. Especially in her memoirs and journals, she has gathered a devoted audience, an audience that has often made her the friend it does not really know but thinks it knows through her memoirs and journals. These nameless readers are distant yet intimate companions of her daily routine and come to her memoirs and journals again and again to be restored. There will always be the academic critic who finds this appeal unacceptable for scholarly response; the same critic, however, may well choose a Sarton journal to hand to a friend who confronts loneliness or sudden despair. The appeal of Sarton is very real; countless readers attest to it.

As popular as the memoirs and journals remain, it is as a poet that Sarton most wishes her reputation to stand. The many volumes of poetry attest to her lifelong commitment and the strength of the verse lies in the adherence to form, in the presence of themes that are sustained throughout the verse, and in the subject matter that deals with women's lives, with love, with the agony of loneliness, with death, with the ever-renewing earth.

Although Sarton has published fifteen short stories, she has not chosen to collect them as a group, and I have chosen not to include them in this study of her major work. She has also done translations (particularly of Paul Valéry with Louise Bogan), but they are not treated here.

The introductory chapter attempts to place Sarton in the rich cultural milieu of her life, to indicate how serious her early days in the theater were, and to suggest the complicated life she lives. I discuss Sarton's work within the genres themselves—memoirs and journals, novels, poetry—concentrating on the singular issues that she has willingly claimed as her own. Because the number of published volumes is large, it has not been possible to treat the work volume by volume.

Instead I have attempted to distill the themes and to trace the development of these themes throughout her work.

Finally, I trust that this brief study properly acknowledges May Sarton's contribution to the world of art and letters. In the steady production of her work she has taken her talent seriously and has used it well. And if she has not enjoyed the critical acclaim she has always hoped would be hers, the work has touched the lives of readers. That, in the end, may be the most important contribution of all.

Elizabeth Evans

*Georgia Institute of Technology*

# Acknowledgments

Grateful acknowledgment is made to May Sarton for permission to quote from the Papers of May Sarton and from the Papers of George Sarton held in the Henry W. and Albert A. Berg Collection, New York Public Library, Astor, Lenox, and Tilden foundations. Special gratitude is extended to Dr. Lola L. Szladits of the Henry W. and Albert A. Berg Collection for assistance and advice as I worked in the May Sarton Papers and the George Sarton Papers. I am grateful to the Berg for permission to use these materials and to quote from them in this study.

I am grateful for permission to quote from the Papers of Louise Bogan held in the Amherst College Library; to Ruth Limmer, Trustee, Estate of Louise Bogan; and to John Lancaster of the library.

Excerpts from these poems are reprinted by permission of Russell & Volkening, Inc.: "Monticello" copyright 1941 by May Sarton, renewed © 1968 by May Sarton; "Poet in Residence" from *The Lion and the Rose* copyright 1948 by May Sarton, renewed © 1976 by May Sarton /as for "Spring Song" and "My Sisters, O My Sisters"; "In Time Like Air" © 1956 by May Sarton, renewed © 1984 by May Sarton.

Excerpts from *The Single Hound* by May Sarton are reprinted by permission of Houghton Mifflin Co. Copyright 1938 by May Sarton, renewed © 1965 by May Sarton.

Excerpts from *Encounter in April* by May Sarton are reprinted by permission of Houghton Mifflin Co. Copyright 1930, 1932, and 1937 by May Sarton, renewed © 1964 by May Sarton.

W. W. Norton has most kindly granted permission to quote from the works of May Sarton published under their imprint.

An excerpt from *The Complete Poems of Emily Dickinson,* edited by Thomas H. Johnson, is reprinted by permission of Little, Brown and Co., copyright 1914, 1942 by Martha Dickinson Bianchi.

I am grateful for the diverse and excellent editorial advice from Professor Warren French, Liz Traynor, and Barbara Sutton.

I am especially indebted to Eric Swenson, May Sarton's editor, for permission to quote his letters to May Sarton concerning the publication of *Mrs. Stevens Hears the Mermaids Singing.*

I am grateful to the Georgia Tech Foundation for a grant that allowed the manuscript research for this study.

# Chronology

1940    *Trelawney* (a play) produced at Concord Academy; begins annual lecture/poetry-reading tours.

1943    Organizes poetry readings at the New York Public Library.

1946    Serves as poet-in-residence, Southern Illinois University; *The Bridge of Years* (novel).

1947    Spends April–July in Europe; *The Underground River* (a play); receives Golden Rose Award (poetry).

1948    Spends April–September in Europe; *The Lion and the Rose* (poetry).

1949    Spends April–August in Europe.

1950    *The Leaves of the Tree* (poetry); *Shadow of a Man* (novel); Mabel Sarton dies.

1950    Spends May–June in Europe; attends Bread Loaf Writers' Conference.

1952    Spends June–September in Europe; *A Shower of Summer Days* (novel).

1953    Named Lucy Martin Donnelly Fellow, Bryn Mawr College; receives Reynolds Poetry Award; *The Land of Silence* (poetry).

1954    Spends August–November in Europe.

1955    *Faithful Are the Wounds* (novel); receives Guggenheim Award and Tidewater Prize.

1956    George Sarton dies.

1957    Spends May–July in Europe; *The Birth of a Grandfather* (novel); *The Fur Person* (tale).

1958    *In Time Like Air* (poetry); nominated for National Book Award in poetry and in fiction; buys house in Nelson, New Hampshire.

1959    Spends June–August in Europe; *I Knew a Phoenix* (memoir).

1959–1964    Lectures at Wellesley College (creative writing, English).

1961    Spends March–July in Europe; *The Small Room* (novel); *Cloud, Stone, Sun, Vine* (poetry).

1962 Marks fiftieth birthday with a trip around the world.

1963 *Joanna and Ulysses* (tale); visits Yaddo.

1964 Spends August in Europe; visits Yaddo.

1965 *Mrs. Stevens Hears the Mermaids Singing* (novel); serves as writer-in-residence, Lindenwood College.

1966 Spends April–June in Europe; *A Private Mythology* (poetry); *Miss Pickthorne and Mr. Hare* (fable).

1967 Spends September–October in Europe; *As Does New Hampshire* (poetry).

1968 Serves as writer-in-residence, Lindenwood College; *Plant Dreaming Deep* (memoir).

1969 *The Poet and the Donkey* (tale).

1970 Spends August in Bermuda and Europe; *Kinds of Love* (novel).

1971 *A Grain of Mustard Seed* (poetry).

1972 *A Durable Fire* (poetry); serves as writer-in-residence, Agnes Scott College.

1973 *Journal of a Solitude* (journal); *As We Are Now* (novel); moves to York, Maine.

1974 Spends September–October in Europe; *Punch's Secret* (juvenile book); *Collected Poems, 1930–1973.*

1975 *Crucial Conversations* (novel); receives Alexandrine Award from College of St. Catherine and honorary degree from Clark University.

1976 *A Walk through the Woods* (juvenile book); *A World of Light* (memoir); receives honorary degrees from the University of New Hampshire, Colby College, and Bates College.

1977 Spends July–August in Europe; *The House by the Sea* (journal).

1978 *Selected Poems; A Reckoning* (novel).

1979 Spends May in England and December in Switzerland.

1980 Receives honorary degree from Nasson College; *Halfway to Silence* (poetry); *Recovering* (journal).

1981 Spends June in Europe; *Writings on Writing* (essays); receives honorary degree from the University of Maine.

1982   Judith Matlack dies, 22 December; *Anger* (novel); serves as writer-in-residence, Colby College.

1983   Receives honorary degree from Bowdoin College.

1984   Spends June and November in Europe; *At Seventy* (journal); *Letters from Maine* (poetry).

1985   *The Magnificent Spinster* (novel); receives honorary degree from Bucknell University; sabbatic from lecture tour.

1986   Cancels spring lecture tour because of stroke; *Letters to May* (letters from Mabel Sarton); receives Maryann Hartman Award from the University of Maine.

1987   *The Phoenix Again* (poetry); resumes lecture tour.

1988   Spends March in England; retires from lecture tours/poetry readings; *After the Stroke* (journal); *Honey in the Hive* (portrait of Judith Matlack); *The Silence Now* (poetry); "In Honor of May Sarton," meeting of the Modern Language Association, 29 December 1988.

## Chapter One
# From Wondelgem
# to Wild Knoll

The biographer of May Sarton will find that she herself has already told much of her life through autobiographical memoirs and journals, books that in the past twenty-five years have brought her an audience of readers who, in learning of her life, have found their own enriched. Particularly in *I Knew a Phoenix* and *A World of Light,* Sarton has related her childhood, early life in the theater, and the lives and influences of family and friends. A constant letter writer, Sarton has added invaluable resources to the researcher and the biographer. Her papers, now housed in the Henry W. and Albert A. Berg Collection of the New York Public Library,[1] span her lifetime through correspondence, allowing the reader to enter the past as events are recounted with candor, as daily life and activities are recorded.

Sarton was first of all the daughter of remarkable parents and she has lovingly presented both their lives in *I Knew a Phoenix.* Her Belgian father and her English mother began their young married life in Wondelgem, twelve miles from Ghent, in a charming house purchased when the considerable wine cellar of George Sarton's father, Alfred, was sold. For May Sarton, the pre-1914 life of her parents was another world—a time of contentment as George Sarton began his life's work, writing the four-volume *Introduction to the History of Science,* and Mabel Sarton pursued her talents as an artist and furniture designer. World War I, of course, ended what must have seemed to this young family an ideal existence. Like countless others, they were forced to flee, first to England and subsequently to America. Their return to Belgium after the war spoke the old story—their house had been occupied, possessions scattered, the garden overgrown beyond recognition. Some few possessions did survive, two of which symbolize much in the lives of all three Sartons. When they returned to survey the scene after the war was over, Mabel Sarton spied in a pile of rubbish a fragile object, miraculously unbroken—"a single Venetian glass on a long delicate

1

stem."[2] The sheer delicacy and beauty of the glass reflect the genteel
life this family lived; its remarkable survival against all odds reflects
the courage of all three. Forced to flee what they loved most, they
picked up life in a new land and because they willed it so, they flourished. When they returned to Wondelgem, they also recovered the tin
box in which—literally as they prepared to flee the invading troops—
George Sarton had buried his notes. Without that recovery, he might
not have been able to proceed with the first volume of his history. This
tin box of notes speaks of the scholarly, academic, intellectual life that
characterizes fully the tone and atmosphere of the Sarton household.

Eléanore Marie Sarton was born on 3 May 1912. Her birth in Belgium imbued her with an affinity for that national heritage. Years later
May Sarton would say that even the Flemish painters were in her blood
because she responded instinctively to their paintings and indeed draws
images from Vermeer, Memling, Pieter de Hooch. Their subjects and
colors struck subconcious chords of recognition. Her "twin," the scholarly review George Sarton founded and named Isis,[3] was introduced to
the academic world in this same year. This pairing has often struck
May Sarton as important, and certainly it shows the dual preoccupation
that possessed the family. They were a close-knit unit, intricately involved in each other's lives; all three were intellectuals who shared
interests throughout a lifetime. From her father's scholarly dedication
and her mother's artistic and domestic talent, May Sarton came to
adulthood with a rich background.

Sarton documents her relationship with her parents in I Knew a Phoenix and in A World of Light as well as in her journals, but perhaps even
more significantly in the hundreds of letters all three wrote to each
other. One needs to study these letters because they are rich with detail
and because they began so very early—when Sarton was five years old.

Throughout their lives, all three members of this family wrote letters to each other whenever they were apart. Recently Sarton selected
fifty of her mother's letters to present this remarkable woman to the
public in Letters to May.[4] Mabel Eleanor Sarton was the most loving of
mothers and in fully accepting her role as wife to a dedicated and
demanding scholar, subsumed her artistic life to his scholarly one. As
a young artist she had painted miniature portraits until a nervous
breakdown left her unable to control the brush in so confined a canvas.
Two of these delicate miniatures hang now in May Sarton's home, witness to Mabel Sarton's talent. Her successful career as a professional
designer of furniture in Brussels virtually ended with the onset of

World War I. In the twenties and thirties she was associated with Margaret Gillespie in Washington where the two women founded Belgart. Here Mabel Sarton designed the embroidery patterns that adorned the singular dresses the business produced and taught the employees how to execute the beautiful patterns. This enterprise brought her money to supplement the family income, money that paid for school and summer camp, household items and vacations. With her talent for color and design Mabel Sarton could transform an ordinary room or garment into an object of enviable beauty.

An undated letter she wrote in 1917—when she was confined after a difficult pregnancy and the birth of her second child, Alfred, who lived only five days—begins Mabel Sarton's letters to her daughter. While the mother's weakened condition ruled her days, the letter tells of the unique bond that united her and her daughter. Mabel Sarton always envisioned an independent life for her daughter and wrote from her confinement, "Little May, you are so dear to us already—shall we someday be very dear to *you?*—be your best friends?—You must help us to know. We will try to love you for yourself and not for us" (*LM,* 1). In adulthood May Sarton consistenly has called Mabel Sarton her best friend, and as long as she lived, Mabel Sarton delighted in her daughter's presence and in each accomplishment.

This mother and daughter shared a deep need for solitude and both responded from the heart to the beauty of flowers. Mabel Sarton writes to May in 1932 from Beirut (George Sarton was at the American University in Beirut to study Arabic, essential to him as he wrote the first volumes of his *Introduction to the History of Science*).[5] The letter speaks of her pleasure in looking at "the greatness of the sea & sky & mountains, & the dear exquisite comfort of flowers and leaves & trees." With a close look, she could give flowers life, personify them: "I brought in just two freshly opened anemones, the stamens yet untouched by bees—they are still filled with raindrops. One is leaning round as if to look innocently at what I am doing" (*LM,* 7).

In a 1945 letter Mabel Sarton discusses her own talent and her decision to relegate her life to George Sarton's ambitions: "I am quite sure I should never have been a real artist, able to execute the pictures & portraits I dreamed of, though I spent many years working hard to that end—but I realized it *before* I married—& replaced it by my free will with much humbler ambitions for myself & by my belief in Daddy—& later in you" (*LM,* 57). Illness frequently interrupted Mabel Sarton's routine, but her radiant presence remained always the center of May Sarton's life. It is impossible to exaggerate her singularity, her abiding gift of herself. As we shall see in the discussion of May Sarton's poetry, Mabel Sarton's death is the deepest wound her daughter has suffered.

The relationship between Sarton and her father was quite different. Letters indicate what a charming man he could be. When his son was born, George Sarton wrote his small daughter what a great responsibility she now must assume. "You know that we cannot always do what we like, and that we have very often to do things which we would rather choose not to do. Your little brother knows *nothing* of that. You will have to help him, and in some ways it will be easier for you than for us. Little Alfred will feel himself much nearer to you than to us. It is *you* that he will try to imitate. I hope you will give him only good examples to follow" (Manuscript letter, 19 August 1917). These responsibilities laid upon a five-year-old child mirror George Sarton's assumption that, regardless of age, everybody exercises discipline and restraint, traits that marked his own life.

It is surprising that he allowed his daughter her freedom at seventeen, for he had expected her to follow a conventional pattern for a professor's daughter—college and marriage. Like his wife, he would glory in May Sarton's successes. But where Mabel Sarton's relation with her daughter was of intimate and constant devotion, George Sarton's letters show that his moods swung from delight to fury. In 1932 when Sarton experienced financial difficulties, her father wrote that he feared her mother and he had allowed her too much freedom and that she had failed. She probably suffered, he suggested, "a fundamental weakness" because her life lacked the discipline of his and he issued characteristic advice: "For success in *any direction* always implies a capacity to surrender present pleasure and take pains *now* for the sake of the future" (Manuscript letter, 26 April 1932). He would write her excoriating letters when she handled money unwisely or loaned it too freely; he let her borrow books from his library but if they were not returned promptly or were taken without his knowledge, he wrote scathing reproofs.[6] Incapable of discussing financial matters with his wife and pursuing his lifelong work with unwavering dedication, George Sarton was the scholar's scholar,[7] but often an unreasonable individual. "Only a future biographer perhaps may be harsh enough," Carolyn Heilbrun conjectures, "to guess how the marriage between these two created the artist May Sarton, burdening her with rage as well as courage."[8]

Sarton has acknowledged the difficult relation that always existed between her and her father, at the same time admiring his scholarly ambition and appreciating his dedication and his charm. She wrote to him in 1937, "Your letter was a treasure. I *do* treasure your letters" (Manuscript letter, 31 October 1937). And his letters could be a delight. In the fifties he often heads a letter with the name of a famous person born on that day—"Pierre Curie 55.05.15" or "Domenico Scarlotti 54.10.26." In 1954 he wrote to Sarton (she was then in Ireland) that the Museum Historiae Scientearum in Ghent planned to devote a display case in his honor. In addition to his books and a portrait, the museum desired "a few 'objets personnel.' What shall I send them, my old slippers, or my penultimate straw hat, or a pipe or two? I cannot send new things and I like the old" (Manuscript letter, 1 August 1954). Once he wrote from Naples in distress because donkeys were beaten "without mercy, but perhaps it is necessary,—otherwise the donkeys would stop still and dream of the day when they carried Jesus into Jerusalem" (Manuscript letter, 24 July 1953). Ever mindful that libraries should be properly maintained, he wrote Sarton in 1955 that she should move her books since she no longer was living at home, 5 Channing Place in Cambridge. He declared, "a living library is cheerful and cheering, but I know nothing more saddening than a derelict library like yours. In the evening quietness I hear it moan like a wounded ghost, and that is very painful" (Manuscript letter, 15 May 1955). He always praised her work, applauded her success; he could write with loving affection of his cats—Rufus, Cloudy, the Harvard Club Cat—charming letters that delight but do not obliterate the stern, overbearing letters he was capable of writing and mailing.

## Cambridge and Her Youth

Sarton's early schooling is unusually important. Once the family was settled in Cambridge, Massachusetts (Dr. Sarton was now associated with Harvard University),[9] May Sarton entered Shady Hill School in 1917 and for the next eight years (with two trips to Europe intervening) she attended this cooperative open-air school where creativity and intellectual engagement were encouraged. It was undoubtedly a stimulating atmosphere; all the children, Sarton recounts in *I Knew a Phoenix,* learned to endure physical hardship (the school was literally open air), profited by being exposed to erratic and independent teaching methods, developed stoic constitutions and imaginative ways of learning and of viewing the world. Sarton returns to these days with affectionate memory, particularly for the teachers who were the greatest influence on her—Katharine Taylor and Anne Thorp. A granddaughter of Longfellow, Anne Thorp was both teacher and friend. It was to capture and honor this woman's remarkable presence that Sarton wrote the novel, *The Magnificent Spinster* (1985), so that, at least in her fictional counterpart Jane Reid, Anne Thorp would be remembered. In 1924 Sarton and her mother returned to Belgium, and for that winter school term Sarton attended the Institut Belge de Culture Française and met another remarkable teacher, Marie Closset (who published as the poet Jean Dominique). The Institut, Closset, and her close companions Marie Gaspar and Blanche Rousseau figure prominently in Sarton's first novel, *The Single Hound* (1938). Shady Hill had demanded independent inquiry of their young students; Marie Closset's approach demanded respect for and mastering of the text as text. Nevertheless, the experience in the Belgian school gave Sarton an essential experience for a poet: I learned there, she writes, "to respect the exact, instead of the almost exact, word" (*P,* 130).

## "Be nonchalant"

The lively years at Shady Hill School ended with eighth grade graduation in 1926 and Sarton then entered Cambridge High and Latin School from which she graduated three years later as class poet and winner of the French prize. Her parents were in Europe when she graduated from Cambridge High and Latin, and Sarton seems not to have regretted their absence, perhaps because she was pleased to be done with formal schooling. She wrote to them cheerfully on 8 June 1929 that she had won the French prize ("a marvelous tooled leather edition of 'Cyrano' in French") [Sunday 9 June 1929]. A week later she wrote that she had also won the Caroline Close prize, which was Stanislavsky's *My Life in Art,* a book she described as "perfectly marvelous," and in the same letter announced that "graduation is over—I am now a dignified alumna of C.H.L.S. and never, *never,* shall I have to go to school again. You can't imagine how happy I am!" (Manuscript letter, 15 June [16? 1929]). These graduation reports also recount (in this same letter) her duties as class poet, particularly her performance at the commencement exercises. "I have never spoken before such a large audience before and it was awfully thrilling!" Sarton has *always* had a sense of her audience, and in 1929 that audience was large and she was thrilled to perform. She was ready—at seventeen—for the New York stage.

The plan, of course, had been for this professor's daughter to enter

Vassar's freshman class in 1929. But when she was fifteen, Sarton and her father saw Eva Le Gallienne in Sierra's *The Cradle Song* and May Sarton fell in love with the Civic Repertory Theatre. So it was to New York as an apprentice with the Civic Repertory that she went at seventeen, not to Poughkeepsie and Vassar. For the daughter of a dedicated scholar to bypass college altogether called for compromise and understanding. As Sarton relates in *I Knew a Phoenix,* her father bitterly opposed her decision and ended family scenes—when the topic was introduced—by banging his fist and shouting, "Never!" Then, without explanation, he capitulated: "It was settled with a little gesture, typical of him, when he and I were standing in the lobby at Symphony Hall at a concert: he offered me a Murad and murmured, 'Be nonchalant.' He then took out of his pocket a letter from Miss Le Gallienne[10] making a definite suggestion that I come to New York the following year. It only dawned on me a few minutes later that he was both admitting me to the grown-up smoking world (up to then I had never smoked a cigarette in his presence) and agreeing to let me have my own way about my profession" (*P,* 149).

For the next six years Sarton's life was absorbed in the theater—with Le Gallienne until the Civic Repertory closed permanently in 1933 and then with her own group, the Apprentice Theatre (renamed later The Associated Actors Theatre, Inc.), which she held together for three seasons until its financial collapse.[11] When her theater failed, Sarton was twenty-four and had to accept this loss. It was, as failure usually is, painful and instructive. These years in the theater were invaluable, and a view of Sarton's life is not complete without taking them seriously into account.[12]

Sarton's letters to her parents give an excellent record of her life in these early years, and what dominates is her commitment to the theater and her capacity to endure the stress of the hard work. Her journey to New York and the Civic Repertory Theatre was no lark, no casual adventure. Her parents, of course, satisfied themselves about her living quarters and often inquired about her routine and her friends. Various letters from 1929 (some bearing full dates, some only the day of the week) are filled with the excited news of her days. "To answer your questions," she writes on a Sunday in 1929, "we have dancing twice a week and fencing twice at 9:45 in the morning until 11. Then we usually have an hour free in which to have lunch and read in the library. At 12 we generally rehearse one of our own plays [the Apprentices] and at 2 the other. Twice a week from 3 to 5 we have voice with Mr.

Brocher as I think I told you. Then of course on matinee days we are free from 2 on and either go to the matinee or home. About twice a week I go to the theatre at night to the plays. This all sounds very regular—but as a matter of fact it varies considerably and is not at all set" (Manuscript letter, Sunday 13 October [1929]). On 3 December 1930 she reports "a day last week" in a letter to her parents.

10:30    *Martine* [play done by the Apprentices] (we are reviving it)
1 P.M.   dress rehearsal ("Alison's House") [This play was based on the life of Emily Dickinson.]
3 P.M.   *Granite* (a student play not cast yet)
8 P.M.   in theater to make-up for *Three Sisters*
11:30–2 A.M.   rehearsal for *Marcellius*

                                                   (Manuscript letter [3 December 1930])

She reported to her parents her various walk-on parts, her roles as a wolf and then as an Indian in *Peter Pan,* and she was thrilled to become a member of Equity when she had some speaking lines in *Living Corpse.* On occasion, Sarton was the prompter ("quite a responsibility," she wrote her parents); sometimes she was called on to usher, and she was even asked once to consult her father on the proper pronunciation of the characters' names in *The Seagull.* The majority of her time was spent in learning roles and in rehearsing; later she filled her role as director of the student group, a role Le Gallienne assigned her in 1931.

During these years she kept monthly accounts of expenditures, submitting them to her parents and trying to live within her modest budget. Whether she maintained or exceeded her allowance is less important than our knowing that her prized purchases, her rushes of extravagance, were books, flowers, and a $35 Victrola. She carefully accounts for her money yet ruefully observes that it goes so fast. Her expense records show some prudence and a habit always of buying books. On one occasion she accounts for the $9.55 that bought *Overtures, Swann's Way, Fathers and Sons, Orphan Angel,* and a subscription to *Poetry.* On another occasion she wrote her mother that she had spent $1.30 on flowers, an abiding passion. "I always glue my nose to the florists on the way home—there are yellow tulips, and pansies, and purple and white anemones—even daffodils" (Manuscript letter, Wednesday [1929]). The flower expense had been recorded, but the bookkeeping was a real effort and not always a successful exercise. She confessed in one letter that she had forgotten to add up the expenses for the previous month; however, she bought a special little book in which she intended to keep strict accounts—from then on.

In 1933 Sarton experienced her most exciting performances in the theater. In April Eva Le Gallienne was ill with bronchitis and Sarton took over her role as Varya in *The Cherry Orchard*. Alla Nazimova (the Russian-American actress known particularly for her Ibsen roles), associated with the Civic, congratulated Sarton; it was praise Sarton happily reported to her parents: "You are extraordinary. It was an excellent performance—words to be cherished" (Manuscript letter, Thursday [Fall 1932]). On another occasion, after spending one night learning the lines, Sarton took over Le Gallienne's role as the White Queen in *Alice*. Le Gallienne was ill, this time with grippe, and Sarton played the role most of an entire week including two matinees. She wrote her parents about her "first real part" and added that Le Gallienne "is letting me use her dressing-room and her maid, so I feel very swell indeed. Last night was like an opening: flowers, telegrams (I don't know how so many people knew!)—it's all great fun—and a swell part" (Manuscript letter, Friday [Fall 1933]). Many years later in her journal, *At Seventy*, Sarton remembers this role. She had telephoned Eva Le Gallienne to greet her eighty-third birthday and the call started the theater memories. Sarton fondly remembered the exhilaration that swept her as a wall of laughter from the audience greeted every line of this role.

While she was succeeding in these roles, Sarton maintained a realistic and modest view of herself and her progress. Again in 1933 she wrote to her parents, describing her current role in an "extravagantly unattractive part" that she played well. Her perception, however, went beyond her performance and interpretation. "I can imagine," she went on, "someone like Nazimova giving it glamour and by her very presence conveying something of nobility—but not someone possessing as little subtlety as young I—so it became sheer melodrama" (Manuscript letter, 14 December [1933]).

During these years Sarton was carried along with the delight and energy the theater embodies. Her performances delighted her. "But O," she wrote her parents, "that feeling of power that I'm beginning to have more and more on the stage—an unrestrained feeling, as if here one would pour oneself out fully into a form without resistance" (Manuscript letter, 28 July [1932]). Sarton's image, "form without resistance," indicates her commitment to her work. The engagement of the acting, combined with her awareness of audience (which she seems always to have possessed), suggest that had circumstances been different, Sarton might well have remained in the theater for life.

Her letters cover her theater years, from those first days as an apprentice with Le Gallienne and the Civic Repertory to the demise of the Associated Actors. Mabel Sarton had followed this latter group with interest and enthusiasm, helping them find housing and securing any number of props and pieces of furniture. In the fall of 1933 the group transported their equipment and props in a twelve-foot-long truck that Sarton said they paid $225 for—and $8 for a heavy tarpaulin. "Apprentice Theatre" had been painted on the door, and she described the whole enterprise to her parents as "snappy." This group had summer runs, engaged in fund raising for their effort (Sarton spoke before several groups in Hartford and in Boston), and had hoped to stabilize as a professional theater group. Sarton admits she could not follow Le Gallienne's advice: one would be wise, Le Gallienne said, "to have won one's spurs in an individual way in the regular (and often horrible) mill of the commercial theatre . . . before starting to fight the windmills of Idealism" (P, 189). Sarton also admits that her stubbornness and her remarkable ability to persuade did not always lead in the best direction. "I was not wise. I was stubborn, convinced that persistence and belief would win out, and, perhaps, unluckily for me, I was still able to convince others. When we disbanded in Hartford, our financial situation was desperate, although our last performances, in which I played Hilda in *The Master Builder,* were sold out." Richard C. Cabot came to their rescue, putting up five thousand dollars to guarantee the group a season in Boston. But their scheduled opening was a disaster as they competed for an audience against the Russian ballet, Katharine Cornell, and, ironically, with Eva Le Gallienne herself. They opened with good performances, but the five thousand dollars was gone in three weeks and the group once again disbanded, this time for good.

What had started at fifteen as a burning love for the stage turned at seventeen into the hard work to realize that theatrical ambition. At twenty-four Sarton was obliged to face and accept the failure. Results of the Great Depression doubtless contributed to the failure, but whatever the causes a significant part of May Sarton's youth had been devoted to an enterprise and an ambition that she could not realize. Years later she looked back upon the experience without bitterness or regret. She left the theater behind, she said, as if she had recovered from the high fever an illness brings. And she has never looked back; her career was not to be on the stage. "Sarton could not," Carolyn Heilbrun argues, "have remained an actress: her dream to play Hilda in Ibsen's *The Master Builder,* while it would have allowed her a grand entrance as a 'new woman,' would also have forced her to function only as an event in the life of a man, the hero of the play."[13] (She had played Hilda with the Associated Actors, but never in a company other than her own.)

As she turned from the life in the theater, Sarton took with her the triumphs and the failures. She also took with her excellent dramatic training—training that has served her well, endowing her with a sense of audience, an awareness of timing, an instinct for character and conflict, an ability to convey emotion, and above all an awareness of the well-modulated speaking voice. For all who have heard her speak in poetry readings, taped interviews, or over the telephone are fully aware of the resonant quality and timbre of the Sarton voice.

The theater years had been full, often hectic. Sarton did spend part of 1931 in Paris, interrupting the New York routine while she lingered to explore Paris until she returned to her duties with The Apprentice Theatre. The letters to her parents reveal that while formal schooling might have ended with Cambridge High and Latin, Sarton's habits of intellectual activity and curiousity had little to do with structured classroom experiences. Her life has always revolved around the stimulation and pleasure that come from books and the discussion of books, from the aesthetic pleasure of flowers and gardening, from music, and from the remarkable friendships she has established and maintained.

Her letters to George and Mabel Sarton written between 1929 and 1932 tell us that, in spite of the theater schedule, she was reading widely and with critical appreciation. Almost every letter to her parents contains good titles, and often she urges them to read what she has just enjoyed. The letters indicate that, having been raised in a house of books and readers, that way of life was natural to her. These letters also indicate that away from home she needed no urging to continue the habit of reading and led herself from book to book to book. At seventeen and eighteen she read widely, commented on style and content, made a stab at learning German (even translating chapters of Matthew). She read biography, some philosophy, and a host of English and European novels. During one period she enjoyed reading French novels so much she did not want to read novels in English. She reported her delight in Shelley's letters and then equal delight in the letters of Keats. Always to whatever her reading schedule was, she added dozens of plays she needed to read as part of her theater education and training. Specific passages in the letters show the maturity of her intellectual life. It is important to note this part of her development and life because Sarton has felt that much of the critical establishment has not regarded her as an intellectual at all.

At seventeen she was an un–self-conscious intellectual. Not surprisingly, the graduation gift from her father was to be a book and she chose, apparently, the one she inquired about in a July 1929 letter: "No news from the Eleanor Duse book? I pine for it" (Manuscript letter, Saturday [27 July 1929]). During the summer of 1929 she reports reading Julian Green's *Adrienne Mesurat,* calling it "a dark book, beautifully written"; she was reading Descartes and in late September noted that she was finishing volume 6 of *Jean-Christophe.* "I'll mail the two I have in my next batch of laundry and would you send me the remaining volumes the same way?" (Manuscript letter, Monday [23 September 1929]). The laundry box would be Sarton's way of borrowing and returning books and phonograph records from and to her parent's house in Cambridge throughout this time in New York. Letters note that she read *Crime and Punishment* and *Fathers and Sons,* bought the *Oxford Book of German Verse,* and read *Swann's Way,* commenting that the style in Proust's book "interests me tremendously. The whole thing told through memory awakened by a sense image. . . . Do read it if you haven't and tell me how you like it" (Manuscript letter, Sunday [3 November 1929]). She read *The Return of the Native* and took a D. H. Lawrence work to the theater to read while she waited for her cue. She liked Galsworthy's *A Modern Comedy* less than *The Forsythe Saga* but added, "I *do* love it. He's so English, so English. And it's rather refreshing after so many Russian and French novels" (Tuesday, [3 December 1929]). She read Mann's *Death in Venice* and *Magic Mountain,* Henry James's *The Ambassadors* (which she did not like because it was "too self-conscious and artificial"), a book of poems entitled *Cry of Time,* her Uncle Ernest's *Types of Philosophy,* and a biography of Leonardo da Vinci. Her request for Christmas in 1930 was for a book— Rachael A. Taylor's *Invitation to the Renaissance* or the book of Sonnets, or a nice edition of *Leaves of Grass* since she had George Sarton's copy of Whitman on loan. But most of all that Christmas she wanted "Katherine Mansfield's essays just published by Knopf" (Manuscript letter, Sunday, [21 December 1930]).

Sarton delighted in Mansfield. With Christmas money she ordered

Mansfield's *Letters* and announced that "they are utterly heavenly. She says things like 'My roses—my roses are too lovely. They melt in the air.' (I *thought* that in French where it sounds sense[14] but in English it's nonsense.) You must read it when I come home" (Manuscript letter, Tuesday, 7 January [1930]). A week later her letter was still full of pleasure with the Mansfield *Letters:* "It's a rare book. I feel as if I had found a new exquisite friend" (Manuscript letter, 14 January 1930). Katherine Mansfield's journal touched her profoundly. "I read a little of K. M.'s journal which . . . is full of arrows which I shall never be able to pluck out of my heart—sentences like these—'When I leave her hands I feel bound with wreaths'" (Manuscript letter, Thursday Eve [26 December 1929]). If this last reaction, as well as some others, reflects youthful enthusiasm more than critical judgment, it remains that Sarton's reading lists and her responses to that reading are impressive for one so young.

She was enchanted with Virginia Woolf, reading *To the Lighthouse* in December 1929 (it had been published in 1927). She was having, she wrote her parents, "a real Woolf mania just now—but I think she is a writer's writer—in the sense that Keats is a poet's poet" (Manuscript letter, Friday [12 December 1930]). She read *Mrs. Dalloway,* which she liked very much, but found *The Waves* a little disappointing. She wrote her mother when she began reading *Orlando* and urged Mabel Sarton to read *A Room of One's Own*—an inevitable choice. Sarton has always reserved a measure of devotion for Virginia Woolf, and when in the thirties she met and spent some time with Virginia Woolf, it was an experience she cherished.

Sarton's intellectual life began early and was shared with her parents. All during the theater years, she was writing poetry and placed several poems—first in *Harp,* and then in *Poetry.* She had occasion to have some photographs made while she was with the Civic Repertory Theatre, and when she looked at them closely she reported to her parents that the image she saw was not that of an actress, but that of a poet. And so it was to be.

## The Literary and Social Milieu

Sarton has gratefully acknowledged her luck in having had excellent friends since her youth, and certainly one of the important friendships for Sarton was with Louise Bogan. The extensive correspondence covers many years, up to mid-1968, two years before Bogan's death. Sarton began the correspondence, and that first letter introduces a topic the two poets discussed frequently: the nature of poetry and the critical reception of contemporary poets. Bogan's executor, Ruth Limmer, has made available much of Bogan's correspondence, in *What the Woman Lived*,[15] but few of the letters to Sarton appear in entirety. A complete reading of both sides of this correspondence is necessary to appreciate the letters. Breaks in the correspondence exist, but enough is available to discover much about the life and work of these two American women poets.

Sarton's first letter is important because it introduces the serious consideration and criticism of poetry. Bogan, as poetry critic for the *New Yorker*, represented the standard in poetry for Sarton who wrote on 21 April 1940, long before she and Louise Bogan met:

> It has been in my mind to write you for some time, to send a word of thanks for your criticism of poetry which seems to stand almost alone in being based on some absolute *poetic* value, some standard beyond belief. I have been watching for reviews of Pitter [the English poet, Ruth Pitter] because this seems to me a test-case. When Spender wrote his very mean review a sort of despair came over me: for the one had said when the really good, the beyond cavil on "the other side" comes along he and his sort will be anxious to prove their integrity by praising it. When this didn't happen I felt the division to be final and real. One would like to feel a sort of brotherhood in the *craft*—but I guess that is a mediaeval idea these days.[16]

The Sarton–Bogan letters discuss the state of lyric poetry and its reception by critics and by the public. In a one letter to Sarton, Bogan mentions "the distrust of form and emotion . . . present in every generation,"[17] indicating the assumed difficulty for the pure lyric poet. Sarton has always preferred to write in form and to capture emotion within her poetry, traits that have invited the distrust Bogan cites. And as poet, Sarton wanted to succeed and had seen the result of the failed poet. She mentions in one letter to Bogan her Belgian friend, Raymond Limbosch, who had tried without success to be a poet. Of Limbosch, Sarton wrote, "I've seen what total unsuccess can do, and it is very much like an illness."[18]

As one would expect, their letters frequently mention other poets they knew and admired: Herbert, Eliot, Yeats, Rilke, Millay, Bishop, Eberhart, Roethke, Rich. In a letter dated 13 November 1953 Sarton rued the death of Dylan Thomas, commenting particularly that the poet who does not suffer early death must recognize that "to have more time is such a responsibility. To use it well, to keep on growing, to be implacably self-demanding and self-critical. . . . I like best to think of poetry as a long life with the best at the end."[19]

Perhaps it is only in *another* writer that a writer can find the critical audience she needs. Sarton relates to Louise Bogan when her work goes well, when the poems will not come at all, when the revision process takes hold, when the reviewers slight her work. Sarton's letters often contained drafts of new poems, and Bogan always responded to this work, usually at some length. She was encouraging but candid. Her remarks on *The Land of Silence* (1953) give useful insights into Sarton's volume and into the criteria Bogan held for poetry. She wrote that Sarton showed her "true maturity" and had "come into yourself and are able to render your mature feelings in your own way." She felt that the volume was too long—"forty poems are enough for a book of lyrics"— and Sarton's contained sixty-seven. Bogan's most significant criticism was a valuable one: she saw certain poems in the volume that seem written as "an *impulse toward literature* [rather] than as direct impulsions from life." Bogan based these comments partly on W. H. Auden's remarks about her own *Poems and New Poems*. Auden intimated, Bogan wrote, "that the world will take play and elaboration and things at second-hand from men more easily than from women. Women must be responsible from the beginning; and women poets are not allowed the latitude that men poets are allowed; they must go to the heart of the matter and *stay* there!—Now, we both know how easy it is to slide into the literary attitude—to let down a little; to repeat oneself and to echo others. Consider Ruth Pitter's later work (get her collected poems and examine them!); and see how she dilutes and repeats, at the end— so that what we read is a kind of lyric *babble,* and no longer poetry at all."[20] Perhaps Bogan's best response to Sarton about *The Land of Silence* came in her comment about the nine poems she considered the strongest. They were poems, Bogan commented, in which "you say what you want to say and then stop! Almost all of these poems approach that shattering impact the lyric must give. To touch, to warm,—to think, to feel—is not enough, as you realize. A lyric poem must be a kind of *flow,* which the poet passes on to the reader almost at the same moment he (she!) feels it himself" (4 January 1954). Bogan's instinct for the pure lyric is well expressed here and embodied in her own poems.

The exchange about poetry was their most important topic, but Bogan and Sarton also wrote freely of their battles with depression. Bogan was twice hospitalized and Sarton has fought depression thoughout her life. Delight in music was yet another exchange, a means for both of pleasure and restoration. As was her habit, Sarton precisely noted the recordings she listened to and recommended. Bogan found such pleasure in music that she renewed piano lessons, happy to find a teacher who pleased her. (Bogan's only child, Maidie Alexander Scannell, graduated from the Juilliard School of Music as a voice major but did not follow a musical career. Bogan's poem, "M., Singing" is but one response to music deeply felt.) And the two poets shared an abiding delight in flowers—Sarton in the garden she nurtured, Bogan, from her New York apartment on 169th Street, enjoying the flowers in Fort Tryon Park as they changed with the season.

Bogan and Sarton did not meet until 1953 and their friendship quickly deepened. Elizabeth Frank in her Pulitzer Prize-winning biography, *Louise Bogan: A Portrait,*[21] argues convincingly that by the mid-fifties, Louise Bogan had so withdrawn emotionally that serious attachments were virtually impossible. (Her two marriages—to Curt Alexander and to Raymond Holden—had ended in divorce; her one successful love affair had gone on for eight years, but it too had ended.) In *Journal of a Solitude*[22] Sarton has described her expectations of the friendship. Sarton's love was immediate and unconditional; Bogan was blocked from,"any exchange of erotic emotion between herself and another woman" from the memories of her mother.[23] Bogan discusses her "mother experience" in a letter to Sarton, dated 2 April 1954, unable to reveal all phases of her traumatic memories and suggesting by withholding that the relationship was complicated. (Her mother's indiscretion with men surely was only part of this problem.) Bogan was willing to encourage, maintain, and enjoy Sarton's friendship, but a serious emotional attachment was out of the question. Her brief letter of 2 April 1954 makes her case. She begins rather matter-of-factly, assuring Sarton that she has no reason to be "terrified of seeing me, for goodness sake!"; next she recommends that Sarton visit Dr. Irvine, Bogan's internist, for help in avoiding the periods of deep exhaustion. Perhaps, like her, Bogan added, "you need extra vitamins." Then the tone becomes more serious as Bogan explains why there will be no emotional, no erotic, attachment:

It is difficult to sum up briefly what I meant about my mother experience. There are certain phases of this experience which I have never told anyone, and never shall. Let me only say that it was too much, and it lasted too long— right through my life up until the age of 39. The most poignant and enduring things in the relationship are in my poetry. The rest exhausted me forever, so far as closeness to the feminine principle is concerned.—I have realized this, because I have thought it all over (and *felt it* over as much as I can allow myself to do) since knowing you; and it has been a good and fruitful thing, on the whole. So *don't* chide me for having opened some doors that I thought shut for good. "The long prose thing," which should be finished by the time I'm 60, should be a final *explication* and *stele*. It is in art that the matter now belongs; not in life. (Manuscript letter, 2 April 1954)

Many of Sarton's letters are as she described them, love letters. Bogan would not return any declaration; she was implacable, unwilling to be moved. She was convinced that once a person had attained maturity, one could not "go back to the childish belief that we can change anyone; or that we can ultimately be 'hurt' by anyone" (Manuscript letter, 18 April 1954).

Their temperaments were different. Bogan carefully calculated her tasks, knew she could never force her poetic life, remained bound to her post at the *New Yorker* both for financial and emotional security. Sarton was energetic, driven to involvements with people, work, causes. Her creative forces were different from Bogan's. They long continued their correspondence, they visited each other, they even collaborated in preparing translations of poems by Paul Valéry (Sarton translated, Bogan "polished"), a project that eventually led to journal publications but not, as expected, inclusion in a complete edition of Valéry commissioned by the Bollingen Foundation."[24]

One of the interesting features of correspondence lies in the particular details, those glimpses that show forth the writer's pleasures and responses to life. These letters are filled with such details, the kind of information that has made May Sarton's journals useful and so appealing. In one letter Bogan told about a party where William Maxwell (a member of the *New Yorker* editorial staff) recited Wallace Stevens's poem "The Virgin Carrying a Lantern." Bogan was struck anew with the poem and added a wonderful detail: "*Harmonium* sold only 100 copies in 1923 and I own one of those bought the week it was published" (Manuscript letter, 13 March 1954)[25]—a testimony to Bogan's good judgment. When Bogan admonished—as she often did—"Sois sage," Sarton replied, "it makes me think of 'Sois sage, o ma Douleur, et tiens-toi plus tranquille' with its wonderful last line 'Entends, ma chere, entends la douce nuit qui marche.'" The quietness of these words are then followed by the lightness Sarton reports from the *New Statesman*: "By the way did you see in the *New Statesman* Roy Campbell's grotesque Gilbert-and-Sullivanish translation of L'Invitation au Voyage? 'My daughter, my sister, / Consider the vista / Of living out there, you and I.' That is all."[26]

The Sarton-Bogan letters are most valuable, of course, for the exchanges about poets and poetry. In addition, this extensive correspondence gives glimpses of daily activities—books read, plays they saw, friends they visited, as well as insight into Bogan and Sarton as women and as poets.

Another of Sarton's most interesting correspondents, especially during the forties and fifties, is the artist William Theo Brown. (The Sarton Papers include 161 letters.) Brown studied at Yale and later at Berkeley, settling in Los Angeles to paint. Brown read Sarton's poetry and novels, thoughtfully giving encouragement and useful commentary. When *The Lion and the Rose* was published, Brown praised the poems, particularly "My Sisters, O My Sisters," and found that the lyrics in this volume represented Sarton at her best. In turn, Sarton praised Brown's paintings, keeping among her papers the handsome twelve-page catalog of Brown's 1967 show at the Felix Landau Gallery in Los Angeles. William Inge wrote the catalog introduction and in his concluding paragraph said that "the paintings of William Theo Brown are comfortable to live with. But one must not be deceived that this comfort is of blindness or indifference to the contemporary world."

Sarton wrote Brown when she bought her first painting, reporting the episode with characteristic narrative flair. She had been in New York, staying at the Brevoort Hotel in May of 1943 and "THE EVENT" of the trip was buying the painting. "It was up at J. B. Neumann's gallery. He is a soft old dear of a Viennese dealer whom I have always loved because he is so un-blasé, a real Amateur in the old sense of the word—he has a gallery called 'Living Art' in the Fuller Building where he mixes everything from New Mexican Santos to Paul Klee up together. And there I beheld a brilliant little scene, like a dream, all in bright colors, of a park in the Bronx which is obviously nowhere—done in crayons and waxed so it shines rather—and it was only twenty-five dollars so I have bought it on the installment plan." The artist, Sarton says, was Isaac Litwak, a cabinetmaker who at age seventy began to paint, ignorant of other artists, but "totally immersed in his own vision" (Manuscript letter, 21 May [1943]).

Brown and Sarton also shared a love of music. Sarton reported that during Christmas 1954 she had bought a record player for her study, pleased now to "play music every morning for an hour before I start to work. It will, I know, make an enormous difference in the daily job of shutting out all the details of life here, and *submerging* if that is the word" (Manuscript letter, 29 December 1954). Brown was thoroughly at home with music; as Sarton put it, he was "really in the world of music" while she was "an outsider who occasionally can get a glimpse through the key hole" (Manuscript letter, 9 April 1942). Brown's letters are filled with anecdotes of his visits with Stravinsky, the most important of which occurred in 1953. Brown stopped by and found Stravinsky and his wife upset by a telegram. They had been expecting one announcing Dylan Thomas's arrival to work with Stravinsky as librettist, but ironically the one that arrived announced his death. Brown spent time with Paul Hindemith and his wife and was great friends with Robert Shaw in whose chorus Brown sometimes sang. Brown was also in the chorus for a performance of the Verdi *Requiem*, which Toscanini conducted, and during rehearsal, in a rage, Toscanini dismissed a member of the orchestra. As the player made his exit, he paused to hurl a string of curses at the maestro who raised his hand in a typical Toscanini gesture and said, "Don't apologize!"

Other musical adventures include a July night in 1951 when a friend took Brown to the apartment of Nathan Milstein where they sat enraptured as Milstein stood and played his Stradivarius until 3:30 in the morning, moving, Brown writes, through music of vastly differing types. Brown wrote Sarton of his delight over spending a weekend at the home of Francis Poulenc outside of Amboise. Poulenc's house and formal garden were set high on a hill, the view of the valley of vineyards and the fruit trees as enchanting to Brown as the music and conversation.

Other correspondence in the forties presents another phase of Sarton's interests, documenting her relief efforts during World War II as she sent parcel after parcel to supplement the limited goods her friends in Europe could obtain. For example, letters to and from the English poet, Ruth Pitter, indicate how much Sarton's efforts meant. The winter of 1940 Pitter described as some frightening sort of spiritual nightmare, the suffering so widespread that Pitter declared it was impossible to shed tears. Tears, she wrote, had simply been left far behind with all of the youth she once had claimed. In April 1942 Ruth Pitter gratefully wrote that Sarton's parcel had reached them, bearing the luxuries of dried apricots, chocolate, tea. On another occasion Pitter told how even the wrapping paper and the string from the parcels were pressed into immediate use. Colored wool threads that had bound some items were given to her nieces for bits of dress embroidery because, Pitter added, there was no such material to be had. Sarton was also sending parcels and letters to H. D. and Bryher (Winifred Ellerman) who quickly conveyed their thanks; however, H. D. and Bryher were far more concerned in 1944 over the devastating conditions that Sylvia Beach was suffering and urged Sarton to enlist the aid of other American writers.

There were also Belgian friends who suffered separation of families as well as limited goods. In Cambridge Sarton endured the days of the war knowing the danger her friends lived with. She wrote William Theo Brown of sending small packets first class—food and soap to the Lombosch family near Brussels—to speed delivery and reported that her friends "the Sparrows whose child was killed by a robot-bomb (my godchild) have now adopted seven-weeks' old twins and I sent off a lot of rubber panties and sweaters and things the other day. One could really spend one's life and all one's money sending off packages these days" (Manuscript letter, 2 March [1945]).

The Sarton Papers give us documentation for many literary friendships that May Sarton enjoyed, engaged in, profited from, contributed to. There are letters from Janet Flanner in Paris who immediately established a comfortable rapport as she read Sarton's work—others from Conrad Aiken, charming letters from Marianne Moore, letters from Muriel Rukeyser, from Elizabeth Bowen to list some of the most familiar names. Sarton's deepest literary friendships are the subject of part 4 in *A World of Light*. There she writes of Louise Bogan. She includes S. S. Koteliansky whose house at 5 Acacia Road in St. John's Wood in London was a gathering place for his friends who included D. H. Lawrence and Katherine Mansfield, both of whom he had championed early and about whom he would hear no criticism. It was Lawrence who called Koteliansky "the Lion of Judah," and for Sarton he was a central influence who read her work and could be depended upon for useful criticism, for friendship. *A World of Light* also recalls Elizabeth Bowen and Jean Dominique. For Bowen, Sarton experiences both love and admiration. Bowen was the model for the lovely artist, Georgia, in Sarton's first novel, *The Single Hound*, and when Sarton wrote *A Shower of Summer Days*, she relived her visits to Bowen's Court as she created her fictional Dene's Court after it. This friendship would last for years and when she visited America, Bowen usually stopped in Cambridge for a stay with Sarton and Judith Matlack. The friendship with the Belgian poet Jean Dominique (Sarton's teacher, Marie Closset) was kept vital by a weekly exchange of letters for twenty years. That long correspondence was, Sarton has said, "A little like what I do now in keeping a journal and perhaps I keep a journal because there is no one any longer to whom I could write such letters."[28]

Letters did carry more than war news and H. D.'s letters often comment on Sarton's poetry. Occasionally, H. D. included some of her own work and claimed that the early titles did not reflect her current self or work. They should be called, she remarked, what Ezra Pound had called his earliest volumes, "visiting cards." H. D. urged Sarton to handle criticism from reviewers so that she was not unduly challenged. What they had to say must not interfere with what she must write. Their letter exchange also shows that they concurred about a primary source of inspiration for their work—old loves.

After the war these connections turned from the painful topics of war and suffering. In 1947 Ruth Pitter wrote praising Sarton's poetry, finding that in equal measure her poems touched the heart and the intellect. In 1950 Pitter reported that her sister had developed into a competent painter, quite to Pitter's surprise. The accomplishment affirmed an important aspect for women, she suggested: it often is after women reach the age of fifty that they come into and claim their life— aesthetically, intellectually, spiritually. And in novel after novel Sarton's women characters do just that.

In one way, the most significant literary friendship for May Sarton was with Virginia Woolf. Although they were by no means intimate friends, Woolf did correspond with Sarton and they did meet several times. Virginia Woolf invited Sarton to tea and when Sarton was occupying the apartment of Julian and Juliette Huxley at Whipsnade Zoo in London's Zoological Gardens, she entertained Virginia and Leonard Woolf at dinner. (In spite of bad weather the dinner went off well, and Leonard Woolf mentioned the pleasure of that evening in a letter to Sarton many years later.) Volume 6 of *The Letters of Virginia Woolf*[29] includes most of the ten letters and postal cards that Woolf wrote to May Sarton in the thirties. Although the letters are cordial enough, it is clear that Woolf is besieged by requests to read manuscripts and new books of promising writers, by invitations, by callers who wanted to see her and talk. Woolf's letter of 2 February 1939 is particularly interesting. Sarton was attempting to gather manuscript pages from writers for auction on behalf of war refugees. Woolf was not disposed to send any since, she wrote, "I tear up my manuscripts when I have any." However, in the end, she did send the manuscript of *Three Guineas* which was sold to an unidentified Miss Jones for, Woolf wrote Elizabeth Bowen, "I hope . . . a large sum." (Woolf's 9 October 1937 letter shows that having to deal with so many visits, including Sarton's, was not altogether easy and she could say so to Bowen with some sharpness.)

Sarton's admiration for Virginia Woolf began early and began as it should—by reading Virginia Woolf's books practically as they were published. It was to be a lifelong admiration, and when Virginia Woolf died, Sarton was deeply moved as her poem, "Letter from Chicago. For Virginia Woolf," attests. In a letter to William Brown dated 23 April [1942] Sarton says she will try to find a picture of Virginia Woolf to send him and remarks about Woolf's appearance. "The rather mad one [photograph] which has appeared in the last reviews doesn't do her justice at all. She was not mad-looking and the last time I saw her her hair was gray and softly curled at the back instead of straight and strange." Sarton's friendship with Virginia Woolf was slight, but to have been associated with Virginia Woolf at all would make a deep impression on almost any writer, as it did on Sarton.

The world of May Sarton includes Europe and America, the academic world and the world of publishing, the travels to many parts of the world, from the "home" bases of Cambridge, Massachusetts; Nelson, New Hampshire; and now York, Maine. That world has included active social involvement like Sarton's 1943 undertaking—a series of poetry readings at the New York Public Library, an attempt to remind people of poetry in the midst of the disruptions of war. (William Carlos Williams, Marianne Moore, and Muriel Rukeyser were among the poets who read.) During World War II Sarton joined others in Cambridge for Red Cross training; she was active in the concerns of the American Civil Liberties Union during the communist hysteria of the McCarthy era and made one radio speech to protest that hysteric reaction. Now at seventy-six, when Sarton says she watches the evening television news because she wants to know what is going on in the world, she is simply continuing her lifelong commitment to know and care about the affairs of the country and the world.

The intellectual and social milieu of May Sarton's life was established in large measure by the habits and tone of the home she grew up in. Those qualities continue today as she lives at Wild Knoll, her house by the sea. Her letters provide glimpses of her daily activities throughout her life, glimpses that let readers experience part of her life. One such glimpse from the past shows how the Sarton household spent

Thanksgiving Day 1941. Sarton's brief description of their activities epitomizes the tone and quality of her life then—and now. She wrote to William Brown on 24 November 1941: "I hated Thanksgiving myself—I hated buying all that food and kept thinking of Belgium—but it turned out to be quite a charming day—Desire Defauw (the conductor) our old friend and also a 'Gantois' from Belgium brought his Stradivarius which someone had just flown across with—and he stood in his shirtsleeves in front of all my father's books and played for hours (we have no piano) and then I read a few American poems—and we finally played records of the Mozart Clarinet Quintet—and it was all very warming and friendly and dear. I love getting glimpses of that pre-1914 life of my parents as I was too young to remember anything of it now—there is no substitute for people you knew at twenty and both my parents blossom and grow visibly younger remembering the wild things they did" (Manuscript letter, 24 November 1941). From her youth, Sarton's world has been rich, and if she has not achieved the acclaim she had hoped her talent would merit, she has touched the lives of readers.

## Chapter Two

# "By This Familiar Means": Memoirs and Journals

It is a tricky business for a fiction writer to attempt autobiography, biography, memoirs, and journals. Even though all these forms involve the *self* and that person's lived experiences, the focus, approach, sense of timing, and emphasis shift altogether. The balance usually is perilous: if the writer "acts too soon, he may seem harsh and insensitive; if he waits too long, the freshness may have faded; he may be tedious."[1] The distance that time allows is advantageous—experiences can be viewed without the pressure they themselves generated; what is remembered and used can be judged and analyzed. Particularly in *I Knew a Phoenix* Sarton produces autobiographical writing that is at once vibrant and controlled. Nowhere else in her entire oeuvre does she quite equal again such skill as here where she recounts her life with sure detachment. From the security of middle age she can afford to call up the aspirations of youth, knowing now both the pleasure and the price of being young.

By middle age she knows the experiences and the memories that persist, those that daily inform and influence. This distance also allows the significant portraits in *A World of Light,* portraits of the seven men and the four women whose friendships shaped so much of her view both of art and of the world. The five of these portraits that appeared first in the *New Yorker* convey the subjects' personalities and strengths without giving way to mere praise or indulgence. The pieces in *I Knew a Phoenix* and *A World of Light* are memoirs requiring Sarton to search both her memory and impressions, to establish the needed factual data, to select and if need be reshape those events to best accommodate the subject as she herself writes in present time. The story of her life in Nelson, New Hampshire, *Plant Dreaming Deep,* also takes this form, a form that allows the writer to rethink as she retells. This process means that she "can filter the harshest details."[2] Like the photograph, the memoir can be tinted or touched up, enlarged or only partially exposed to create closely or at a distance the picture and the impression desired and, like the photograph, "the memoir keeps some outward form, not dishonest but devoid equally of animation and the indifference of time."[3]

These three memoirs share many characteristics, but they are also distinctly different as even their titles show. *I Knew a Phoenix* (1954) bears a second line in the title, "Sketches for an Autobiography." Here Sarton tells her life's story from birth to age twenty-five, from her infancy in the Edenic Belgian place Wondelgem through her girlhood in Cambridge, Massachusetts, her adventure at seventeen into the theater rather than into Vassar's freshman class, and her life with the friends and acquaintances who shared her youth and ambitions. We learn the intriguing stories of her mother and her father (both of whom suffered traumatic childhood experiences); of Marie Closset (the poet Jean Dominique), her teacher during a year in Belgium in 1924; of Eva Le Gallienne whose Civic Repertory Theatre gave Sarton her theater training; of Lugné-Poë, French entrepreneur, director, actor—a talented man Sarton described as "Belasco, the entire Theatre Guild board of directors and Alfred Lunt rolled into one" (*P,* 166); and of the charming friends in England—Julian and Juliette Huxley, S. S. Koteliansky, Elizabeth Bowen, and more slightly, Virginia Woolf. *I Knew a Phoenix* is indispensable autobiography, filled with familiar details and impressions and narrated from a distance that allows control.

Sarton subtitles *A World of Light,* "Portraits and Celebrations," and begins this work with two poets important to her: the Belgian poet Jean Dominique and the American poet Louise Bogan. She includes Elizabeth Bowen who, Sarton says, looked "like a drawing by Holbein" (*WL,* 193). The art allusion captures Sarton's admiration of Bowen; it was a friendship that brought the two writers together in England and in America—a friendship that lasted for many years.[4] The four divisions of *A World of Light* are complements: along with her parents and the writers are family friends as well as two of the talented and remarkable working men she knew well—Marc Turian (A Swiss vigneron) and Albert Quigley (her neighbor and fellow artist in Nelson). These portraits introduce, portray, and celebrate these individuals as contributors to and companions of May Sarton's life.

*Plant Dreaming Deep* (1968), while still a memoir, fulfills quite a different purpose, and it is the book that substantially broadened Sarton's reading public. It brought Sarton to the attention of Carolyn Heilbrun, who has said that here "Sarton achieved something close to a new form for female writing; she transformed the genre, even as she reported a new female experience."[5] What Sarton does is to recount her life from age forty-five to fifty-five, recount the middle age of a woman's life that is not identified by or lived in the traditional roles of wife or mother. Instead, Sarton writes of the woman living alone. When she bought the house in Nelson, New Hampshire, gathered in the furnishings once repairs and remodeling were finished, and then successfully established herself there, Sarton could give her readers "the possibilities of the solitary female life, but without negatively defining the condition of those who are *just* women." The theme of solitude pervades Sarton's work from its very beginning, but with *Plant Dreaming Deep* she created "the narrative about a woman's working solitude," a narrative that many married women read and envied.[6] Sarton knows, but many of her readers have yet to discover, that solitude carries a dark underside of depression. It is a bit like Perseus slaying the Medusa: to have a victor, there must be a victim. To embrace solitude invites depression and that malign state, loneliness. So many readers found *Plant Dreaming Deep* the record of an ideal life that Sarton literally balanced the matter by showing in *Journal of a Solitude* just how threatening the solitary life can be.

Sarton has relatively little to say about the memoir as a distinct form, but she has much to say about the journal as a form. She has written five: *Journal of a Solitude* (1973) *The House by the Sea* (1977), *Recovering* (1980), *At Seventy* (1984), and *After the Stroke* (1988). For Sarton keeping a journal has meant keeping a record that will be published, a different task from the traveler's journal or from the individual who writes in his journal or diary those thoughts destined only for the writer's eyes. *Journal of a Solitude* and *Recovering* were both begun to help her face up to the end of love affairs and the depression the losses had caused. Part of the motivation was self-examination, hoping that the process would help effect a behavioral change. As she begins *Recovering* on Thursday, 28 December 1978, Sarton states outright that in this sustained exercise she hopes "to sort myself out, and see whether I can restore a sense of meaning and continuity to my life *by this familiar means*" (my italics).[7] On 30 November 1979 she is ready to end this journal. In rereading it, she sees that through its entries she has "made a good journey out of depression and rage, and it is time soon to make an end of this means of handling those demons. It has served its purpose" (*R,* 239).

Sarton's journals have been unusually popular; responses come from all ages, not just from middle-aged women. Her journals, however, are risks simply because they invite familiarity from readers who experience the day-by-day routines of the author's life—making beds and meals, filling birdfeeders and shoveling snow, receiving wanted and unwanted guests, exulting in love and despairing in love lost. As Sarton notes in *The House by the Sea,* the journal process remains a very personal record. The journals may well have provided therapeutic value to Sarton; they have also spoken the unspoken for women who could not express anger, deal with regret, welcome the love of women, risk passion in middle or in old age. A role model for younger women and for her own generation as well, Sarton has maintained the balance of a well-written journal and a very personal record, has done so by heeding Elizabeth Bowen's dictum: "One must regard oneself impersonally as an instrument."[8]

Within her journals Sarton refers to the actual writing process. In *The House by the Sea,* for example, she describes the journal as a good way to sort out and shape experience "at a less intense level than by creating a work of art as highly organized as a poem, for instance, or the sustained effort a novel requires" (*HS,* 27–28). Sustained journal writing, however, makes its own demands. Travel, even a short two days away, breaks the thread and makes picking up difficult. Long trips can interrupt the daily recording altogether, as can the disruptions of illness, holidays, guests. Because each journal entry is dated, the literal turning of the calendar creates pressure to get the work done. To achieve its sense of freshness, the journal is written, Sarton frequently says, "on the pulse" and "must be concerned with the immediate, looking back only when the past suddenly becomes relevant in the light of the present moment."[9] It is, Sarton declares in *At Seventy,* "the business of the journalist to record a mood as it comes, as exactly as possible, knowing that life is flux and that the mood must change" (*S,* 34).

At times the journal has literally been a way for Sarton to pace herself: partly wanting to verify that something is finished each day and partly because "keeping a journal again validates and clarifies" (*S,* 50). She is keenly aware of the journal's limitations, calling it a minor kind of creation yet also aware of its demands. Journals written on the pulse must be concerned with the immediate, and the immediate which allows little reflection, affords little distance, and inevitably includes the banal—those ordinary activities that must be dealt with but that are not the moments of the artist's inspiration. By habit, Sarton records the routine of her day—waking time, house chores, writing time, gardening, resting, cooking. Her reading habits are also recorded as she cites book titles, occasionally copies out passages, discusses the impact a title or author has had on her. When Sarton copies out the action of mercy passage from Flannery O'Connor's story, "The Artificial Nigger," she shares her admiring response to that passage with the reader.

When Sarton listens to music, she notes what piece of music she played, cites the composer, the artists, the record number. And she has done so since her early days in New York when she depended on loans from her father's record collection for music. The journal entries reveal that in emotional distress or during radical change, Sarton cannot listen to music. She mentions in *The House by the Sea* that she could play musical recordings only after she had fully settled into the large house, Wild Knoll, on the Maine coast—a process that required a year and a half. Earlier when she had moved from Cambridge to Nelson, New Hampshire, she had to adjust and sense how different types of music struck here with the changing sesons in that rural place. Hearing Bach, Mozart, Vivaldi provides Sarton with clarity and structure; hearing a Mozart quintet can "air things a bit." This careful listening was part of the routine that her parents observed. Indeed, George Sarton noted precisely what he listened to and mentioned those facts in letters. May Sarton knows, for example, that in the month after her mother died, her father found some comfort in recordings of Dvořák, Gluck, Beethoven, Brahms, Palestrina, Stravinsky, Chopin, Pergolesi. Music has been a link with her parents, a source of solace in itself, and a source of allusions and analogy that provides connections, harmony, resolution. Her descriptions frequently center in musical imagery. Hanging the portrait of her ancestor, Duvet de la Tour, in her Nelson house "was on a note of triumph, as if a piece of music where many themes have been woven together was just coming to a satisfying close".[10]

Another motif throughout the journals is Sarton's deep-felt response to nature, especially now to the thunderous sea and the grassy meadow that form the natural boundary of her house in York, Maine. Like her mother before her, creating a garden of flowers is a necessity. The work and pleasure begin on winter days when she peruses plant/seed catalogs and continues in the daily summer chores of weeding and watering. The flower garden makes up part of the morning routine: cutting, arranging, placing flowers throughout the house, a particular arrangement enhancing an entire room. Journal entries range wide, but through them all what the reader discovers is a writer at work and consciously aware of the journal as a form. Sarton's intent in beginning and ending a journal and in exposing raw nerves reflects her candor. The reader knows her daily routine, invited to do so by the journal pages themselves. And this very knowledge invites intrusion as many move from the facts and presume friendship. Sarton naturally resents the intrusion of the public yet the very nature of her journals invites that same intrusion. The exposure and the private self: the balance is precarious, the price to keep the balance sometimes high.

Each of the five journals covers roughly one year. *At Seventy* is exactly that, beginning on Sarton's birthday (3 May 1982) and ending on 2 May 1983. (*At Seventy* and *After the Stroke*, the two journals of her "old age" both, ironically, are begun in the spring of the year.) Sarton is explicit about the keeping of a journal. Because the journal can be "too easy, too quick, perhaps," there is the obvious danger of "bending over oneself like Narcissus and drowning in self-indulgence" (*R*, 77; *HS*, 78). For this reason, Sarton says the young should not keep a journal because they lack an adequate sense of self, are too tempted to self-indulgence, to be the recorders and keepers of journals, especially a journal destined for the public's eye. The keeping of a journal is harder than it looks as Sarton describes the process in *The House by the Sea*: "If a journal is to have any value either for the writer or any potential reader, the writer must be able to be objective about what he experiences *on the pulse.* For the whole point of a journal is this seizing events on the wing. Yet the substance will come not from narration but from the examination of experience, and an attempt, at least, to reduce it to essence. Secondly—and this is curious—what delights the reader in a journal is often minute particularities" (*HS*, 78–79).

Although Sarton's entries are dated and give the impression of daily work, she does not write an entry every day as a rule and does not believe that one can. Entries also vary in length—some are less than half a page, others extend for several. At times, a subject from a book read or from a guest's conversation becomes the subject for entries over several days. All the journals spring from her need to record and sort out experience. Autobiographical writing, she says, springs from "'what I remember' whereas the journal has to do with 'what I am now, at this instant'" (*HS*, 79).

Some aspects are common to all of the journals. Sarton records the date and usually the prevailing weather. She will note the visits of neighbors and friends, household chores and shopping, professional life outside the study (poetry readings, lectures, interviews), her reaction

to political and social issues. She will cite the music she has listened
to and she will brood over the illness of some friends, the deaths of
others. A central part of her routine and of the journals focuses on
animals. For sixteen years her dog, Tamas, was a constant pleasure; and
the wild cat she named Bramble and domesticated was much prized.
(These two animals died in 1987, the hard year when Sarton herself
suffered a stroke. Only those who love animals can respond to the
sadness that comes when they die.) Throughout the journals Sarton
examines her own psychological makeup and behavior—the bouts with
depression, the scenes of anger and rage, the restoring of relations with
self and with others, the lack of serious critical attention to her work
as poet and novelist. She also records details of her own health, especially when illness or accidents frighten her and interrupt her work
schedule. And the last two journals explore an especially important
topic—the process of growing into old age.

A theme recurring in the memoirs and the journals is the figure of
the writer who must write, first since that is her calling and second
because that is her means of livelihood. A college professor, Sarton
says, can connect with her class, can spark interest, cause reactions,
and thus stimulate her own work. "The writer, at his desk alone," she
argues, "must create his own momentum, draw enthusiasm up out of
his own substance, not just once, when he may feel inspired, but day
after day when he often does not" (*PD,* 58). Key parts of Sarton's life
and work, explored in the memoir and journal pages, converge in this
passage. There is the reality of a woman alone making her living in
the difficult and uncertain role of writer. Sarton has not gained financial security through inheritance or by producing best-sellers. Her reality is that of a single income that depends upon her steady production.
And her first love, poetry, could not provide adequate income nor be
produced at will. Whatever the progress of the pattern of the poet in
America, few if any have made their entire livelihood by it. (The poetry
circuit of readings about the country—"Poe-bis," as Maxine Kumin
calls it—supplements poets rather than fully sustaining them.) For
Sarton, the success and popularity of the memoirs and journals have
made a financial difference, an important fact for one who has not had
a tenured teaching post. She has produced steadily because she has had
to, generally a book a year. She must be mindful of the New England
winters and the heat bills they cause and mindful as well of yearly
income taxes—facts of life she often mentions within the journal pages.

Both in *Plant Dreaming Deep* and in the journals Sarton records her anxiety over reviews. An entry in *The House by the Sea* notes that *A World of Light* will be published in a few weeks, and Sarton says that event will bring a week or so of pleasure until the reviews appear and the inevitable shredding begins. When *Kinds of Love*, her New England novel of love in old age, was published in 1970, Sarton admits in the journal entries that she was almost overcome with the hope that this novel would make the best-seller list. Although many reviewers praised the novel, it did not make the list and suffered in fact at the hands of a critic like Richard Rhodes who reviewed it for the *New York Times*. [11]

In an alarming way the memoirs and the journal entries contain Sarton's expectation that reviews will be unfavorable. In *Plant Dreaming Deep* she declares that the ghost of failure brings increased anxiety when one reaches middle age simply because there is so much less time to recover and to try again for success. In this memoir she cites four causes that have kept her work from gaining a wide critical reception: her divided loyalty between poetry and fiction, self-indulgence, laziness, and an aspect of failure "written into my very bones" (*PD*, 88). These causes are real to her. It is difficult for one writer to excel both in poetry and in fiction, and her divided loyalty has also meant a division of creative energy. The matter of self-indulgence may account for the coolness some critics have shown when that self-indulgence led to a style that draws attention to itself or allows for too much self-exposure. Laziness cannot be taken seriously since Sarton's impressive list of titles denies the trait in her. Her feeling that failure is written in her bones reveals a despair that anticipates disappointments and unfavorable reviews. In *Journal of a Solitude* she attributes the "repeated blows" from critics and the lack of serious critical attention to her own destiny: "I am not meant for success . . . in a way adversity is my climate" (*JS*, 65). Few writers remain unconcerned about their critical reception, and for Sarton publication and critical response are tied not only to her need for recognition as an artist but also her need for financial success.

Many of her novels especially have had good reviews, and many of Sarton's journals and novels have reached a diverse audience. She recounts in *At Seventy* the story of a plumber named Webster who, when he completed the work he had been hired to do for her, asked that his payment be a signed copy of her novel *A Reckoning*. Reading that book had helped him deal with his wife's recent death. Sarton's numerous letters from fans multiply this story with their own versions of Webster's story. The lives of many readers have been touched by Sarton's work, but this appeal and response are not evidence reviewers often use.

Occasionally a journal entry notes Sarton's progress in a current novel or poem revision. By drawing together this group of comments from the journal pages, one learns first that her full work pattern is not simply the daily routine she frequently describes but—like any professional writer's—it includes a continuous process of finishing one book and struggling to find her way into the next one. When *A World of Light* is finished, she notes in the spring of the next year that at last the beginnings of a novel are stirring. She must guard against pushing too fast, knowing that once the leading character's name is secure, that character will begin to take shape and the novel will slowly follow. In January 1978 Sarton dreads "the effort of getting into the novella, now twenty-one pages long. Of course the first fifty pages are the hardest, when everything has to be invented, the scene itself, the characters, their backgrounds" (R, 38). She notes the specific difficulties she has in writing when she fails to concentrate on detail or fails to bring a scene alive in concrete terms. (Scenes in *Anger* show she can succeed in vivid detail and bring forth scenes in concrete detail.)

In *At Seventy*, written during 1982–83, Sarton reflects on the letters that her novel *Anger* brought. "The book" she writes, "whatever its faults—and I begin to see them now—is reaching people. Writing it I learned a lot about myself and about Ned . . . and it looks as though the readers, too, are being lead [*sic*] to self realization" (S, 194). She makes note in this journal that she was struck by John Cheever's remark: writing is a continuous way to make sense of one's life and discover one's usefulness. Sarton says here that "Every one of my novels has been an attempt to do this, and of course the journals are exactly that in a far easier and less exacting form" (R, 193). The reader should watch the author of a journal present herself in various stages of exposure and discovery—that is the nature of the genre. Sarton reveals that she wrote *Anger* during a year of self-doubt, and through that writing process came to much self-knowledge. Personal issues in her life have led to some of her most successful and convincing work. The journal pages trace the path for us, often in an ingenious way.

Issues that Sarton values spur some of her most effective novels, and journal entries discuss those issues, often as the novel is in progress. In *Kinds of Love* she writes of love in old age; in *The Poet and the Donkey* she portrays the Muse as essential for the poet's work; in *As We Are Now* she deplores ill-run nursing homes where the old and the sick are victims. Her outrage and grief over her Nelson neighbor, Perley Cole, is documented in this novel that one critic called a powerful indictment of the nursing home staffed and run without regard for humane standards. The journal pages allow a much greater intimacy than can the pages of the novel, at least intimacy that touches the writer. The journal allows the writer, if she chooses, to be boldly personal; the novel (generally) asks that the writer be self-effacing. In *Recovering* Sarton says that "in the end as a novelist I have wanted to communicate a vision of life, to project my own ethos, not beat down someone else's" (*R*, 159). This may well be an unconscious motive for all serious writers, but Sarton's journal statement suggests that she has sometimes been too conscious of projecting her own ethos into the novels by stating them so directly. Her views are powerful enough to emerge from imagined characters, and when they do, the effect is far greater than it is through narrative declarations.

In *Recovering* Sarton looks back on the novels she has written up to that time, 1980. "But I still believe that a few of my novels will prove to have value in the end. *Mrs. Stevens, Faithful Are the Wounds, As We Are Now,* and possibly *A Reckoning,* when it comes to be read in depth, and what I actually *said* becomes clear" (*R*, 77). *A Reckoning* should indeed be read carefully and along with *Anger* is an important novel in the Sarton canon. The journals provide Sarton time for intense musing on her own work. What we find is a novelist who has, in spite of everything, stayed at her task, has avoided repetition and imitation, has persistently written of strong women characters who face themselves and the world with independence and courage.

Sarton frequently discusses poetry in the memoirs and journals, centering on two topics: the indispensable muse and her own demands on the poet and the poem. For Sarton, the presence of a feminine muse has been a literal fact, and she has consistently explained that for her the muse is essential if poetry is to be written. The muse, always a woman for Sarton, does focus the world for her, provides the inspiration. The muse may be the partner in a love affair, or she may not; but the power of the experience elicits the poems. Sarton insists that "poetry does not happen for me without a muse. That truth is frustrating often, but it is the truth and has been the truth for the past sixty years at least. It may be that you who ask me that question must accept the fact. What for you may seem like failure (surely if I was grown up enough I could be my own muse is what is implied) for me is mystery, and I am very glad that there is still a real and not-to-be-analyzed

mystery in my life. *Je ne regrette rien"* (*S,* 304–5). This probably is
Sarton's strongest statement about the muse. She takes the mystery for
what it is and constantly attributes her poetry to the presence of a muse
who inspires her.

The journal pages also record Sarton's expectations of poet and of
poem. Distance and detachment from the experience are essential. "We
are permitted," she writes in *Journal of a Solitude,* "to become detached
only after the *shock* of an experience has been taken in, allowed to
'happen' in the deepest sense. Detachment comes with examining the
experience by means of writing the poem" (*JS,* 143). Sarton often
achieves the required detachment by writing in form—especially in the
short lyric and the sonnet. Mindful that writing lyrics and writing in
form are not fashionable, she defends her use, defends it at some length
in *Recovering*: "Meter is how the body still gets involved on the subconscious level. We no longer dance to poetry or as we listen to it, but
way below the conscious level, the beat opens doors" (*R,* 112). Journal
entries also record what Sarton dislikes in poetry—its being too abstract and generalized, its missing the strong metaphor, its being too
theatrical or too self-indulgent. "Poetry is revolting," she insists, "unless it is good poetry" (*HS,* 94).

To Sarton, the "rarest and most precious kind of poem" is the simple
lyric that achieves the greatest spontaneity and uses the simplest words
(*R,* 142–43). When poems are confessional or depend on bravado, they
embarrass. What the poem must achieve is centered in a key word for
Sarton—transparency. This characteristic neither shocks nor calls attention to itself. Instead it leads the reader to look through poet and
poem "and find everyman, yourself. Somewhere between the minute
particular and the essence lies the land of poetry" (*JS,* 97). Katharine
Taylor, a remarkable teacher at Shady Hill School, taught Sarton as a
young girl an indispensable premise: the essence of poetry is self-dis-
cipline, not self-indulgence (*P,* 139). And certainly, as Sarton notes in
several journal entries, an important function and possibility of poetry
is "to make the unbearable bearable and to release grief" (*R,* 57). Links
between journal entries about poetry and Sarton's own poems are easy
to make, and in many of her successful poems one sees these basic
responses at work—particularly so in "In Time Like Air," "Gestalt at
Sixty," and "A Hard Death" to name but three where the reader sees
Sarton exercise a distance from the purely personal as she creates poetry
that speaks of timeless experiences.

Journal pages also recount many reports and details of Sarton's

health, and her emphasis on this topic is probably no more excessive
than that of most journal keepers and writers of letters. (Certainly
Henry James's early letters from Europe to his parents give a minute
and daily account of his health—and lack thereof.) Of particular interest are Sarton's facing and recovering from a mastectomy (*Recovering*)
and her recent stroke and heart problems recounted in *After the Stroke*
(1988). Her sheer endurance in the face of illness is reason enough to
read these pages, and the reader is struck by her ability to persevere.
Only in *After the Stroke* when illness debilitated her for months does
she voice discouragement that seems permanent. But at last as this
journal draws to a close, Sarton has recovered from the stroke, able to
resume much of her normal schedule. Stronger and relieved to be herself again, she resumed work, including a trip to California for poetry
readings, an occasion she has described as "my last hurrah."

In *Recovering* Sarton devotes relatively little space to the mastectomy.
Significant and traumatic, the mastectomy is recorded, contemplated,
assimilated. This surgery did not prompt the journal, but Sarton does
document the event and explores confidently a fear that every woman
has. "What the mastectomy does to each individual woman is, at least
temporarily, to attack her womanhood at its most vulnerable, to de-
value her in her own eyes as a woman" (*R,* 131). Sarton treats this
intensely female experience openly, considering it, for her, an ironic
relief, "for I know that the amount of suppressed rage I have suffered
last fall had to find some way out" (*R,* 117). In her period of recuper-
ation Sarton discovers that "physical disability rouses the will, so much
so that extra power seems to be given in overcoming it, power beyond
what is needed . . . whereas depression, mental anguish, destroy the
will or numb it" (*R,* 128).

In and of themselves, these entries of Sarton's continue to make a
singular contribution—the narrative of a woman's solitude and the narrative of intimate experience that all women face literally or in their
nightmares. In *At Seventy* and *After the Stroke* Sarton has faced the inevitable difficulties of old age and extreme illness as a woman living
alone. Because she herself has always had older friends of vigor and wit
as her models, she has looked forward to old age. However, the reality
of even a mild stroke launched her into old age, she has said, for the
first time. On the first *manuscript* page of *After the Stroke* she writes, "I
am too vulnerable to all the losses and often the pain connected with
personal relationships. . . . It is too complex, too terrible, too astonishing and so the wave of memory dashes itself against rocks." Sarton

edited this passage so that the finished version (dated Wednesday, 9 April 1986) reads: "I am too vulnerable to all the losses and often the pain connected with personal relationships." In her previous journals, Sarton had let daily entries stand as they were written, but the stroke she suffered made her so ill during the writing of the first half of *After the Stroke* that revisions were often needed. While the revised version reads more smoothly, one regrets losing the powerful image from the manuscript—"the wave of memory dashes itself against rocks."

The reader is drawn in this most recent journal, into Sarton's experiences: the support of loyal friends, the daily fear and anxiety, the humiliations that come with medical care and hospital routine. It is, however, the play of memory that fascinates and creates the essence of this journal. The sense of loss as one faces loss is conveyed with feeling. More important, Sarton records the slow recovery from a stroke, an experience many have had but few have described. As some strength returns, she savors the mundane tasks simply because at last some strength has returned. She can smooth out a sheet, manage the stairs, walk the dog. The stroke forces awareness of what Sarton calls the "other inside of the body." Unlike her character Cornelius (*Kinds of Love*) whose recovery from a stroke is limited and far from complete, Sarton's recovery has been excellent even though heart problems still cause grave concern. *After the Stroke* ends with celebration: "So this is the anniversary and I am well! It has been a long journey, but now I do not think about the past at all."[12] Sarton has, I think, wisely tempered what many may have perceived as a "grow old along with me" state. *After the Stroke* documents vulnerability, suffering, despair, and shows us a woman meeting those demons courageously. Her reviewer in the *New York Times*, Nancy Mairs, praises the journal: "Living beside her in her illness 'moment by moment,' as the nature of a journal demands, chastens and deepens the reader's spirit."[13] Mairs has struck a note for all of Sarton's work, not simply for this latest journal. A careful reading of Sarton does chasten and deepen the reader's spirit—if she will read, if she will let it.

Journal entries, of course, record Sarton's private and public successes—receiving honorary degrees from some half dozen colleges and universities (not bad, Sarton likes to quip, for a high school graduate), giving poetry readings to standing-room-only audiences, being the subject of documentary/interview films. In 1983 Sarton agreed to sign books at a feminist cooperative in Cincinnati. There appeared, she writes, "a subway crush of young and old . . . crowding to get *Journal*

*of a Solitude* signed (that is the one for the young and of course *Anger.* . . . And on the way back to the Regency [hotel], . . . two women
from the cooperative told me that they thought they had sold $1,500
worth. . . . It cannot be denied that it is these days a very good life
for an old raccoon of seventy" (*S,* 210). It is interesting that Sarton's
novel-in-progress involves the importance of feminist bookstores as a
place for women to meet—all manner of women—and to serve as a
central unit in the lives of many.

With the publication of *Mrs. Stevens Hears the Mermaids Singing*
(1965) Sarton publicly avowed her homosexuality, identifying herself
with Mrs. Stevens. This novel—and her work in general—may be seen
as radical, she declares, in a "nice, quiet, noisy way" (*JS,* 90). But
Sarton recognizes in *Mrs. Stevens* and in herself the difficulty for lesbi-
ans and contrasts Willa Cather's "stern privateness" with Virginia
Woolf's open admission in *Orlando.* Sarton's ability to be open in the
journal pages has made her a central figure for women's groups and for
individual women who have discovered truths about themselves that
they had difficulty claiming. Many feel compelled to tell Sarton their
story, and most of them see in May Sarton the positive role model, see
her, as she says of herself, "as an acceptable, dignified old woman who
can accept the love of women as the creative spur for herself and who
has written openly about it" (*R,* 154).

When a letter arrived calling Sarton the ur-mother of women's lib-
eration, she rejected such an assumption. Indeed, her association with
the movement has been marginal, but not unsympathetic. She acknowledges that the acts of the most radical women have served to
heighten awareness and to underscore the dilemmas many women face.
Sarton rarely sees a woman continue to create successfully after she
marries and has children. Her view of men, however, has never been
hostile, even though she resents the unjustified deferring to men that
women do on many occasions—consciously and subconsciously. If there
is an ideal state for women, Sarton would say that it occurs when
women understand themselves as *central,* not peripheral; when women's
instincts for nurturing and for self-preservation coexist; and when
women can vigorously find their "true self with or without men, but
not *against* men" (*HS,* 225; my italics). This is what Sarton means by
women creating their own mythology, and it is that state of independence, not hostility, that she expresses in "My Sisters, O My Sisters,"
a poem that ends with a reflection of shared greatness: "For we shall
never find ourselves again / Until we ask men's greatness back from

men / And we shall never find ourselves again / Until we match men's greatness with our own." Matching greatness need not be combative, and it is this position that Sarton has persistently maintained. Her patience is thin when poetry written by women centers in self-indulgence or in mere confession or in shocking details for the sake of exposure. Poems that say, "Look at me, I'm in pain," she argues, are usually not poems.

The key words—transparency, vulnerability, acceptance, honesty— are Sarton's hallmarks in her work as in her life. Amid the plethora of material about the Bloomsbury group, Sarton's recent reflection deserves notice. She sees the strength of the Bloomsbury group centering in "their fantastic honesty about personal life. They accepted that in a given lifetime there are going to be many and complex relationships that nourish and many kinds of love. . . . If they were neurotics, and perhaps they were, they were civilized and civilizing neurotics. . . . Maybe the gossip, incessant, witty, and sometimes malicious, occasionally offends our sense of decorum—with reason. But decorum seemed to them, no doubt, altogether a matter of *how* things are done, not *what* things are said or done" (*JS*, 76–77). Sarton has always risked much, has been willing, especially through the poetry and the journals, to give herself away, to keep few secrets. In doing so, she has maintained always an honest sense of *how* things are done, how the honest life is lived, regardless of social standards that tolerate no breach.

## Solitude—My Last Great Love

Perhaps only Thoreau and those in religious orders have written about solitude as movingly as has May Sarton. For her, solitude has always been central, demanding, essential. In 1973 she published *Journal of a Solitude* partly, as we have seen, to dispel a public response that had judged her solitary life in *Plant Dreaming Deep* the idyllic state. Solitude, she argues, brings its dark side of panic and depression, but Sarton in living as and writing about the woman living alone has persistently elevated solitude without sentimentalizing it. She learned it early, remarking in *I Knew a Phoenix* about her life in London during the spring of 1936: "I am aware that the words 'alone' and 'solitude' and even 'loneliness' keep appearing on these pages. They have the sound of happiness about them, and in fact, being alone was one of the major reasons why I was happy" (*P*, 201). Solitude increases one's perception since distractions are fewer; solitude becomes richer for Sarton as violent romantic attractions subside. Solitude is the essential respite and function to balance the stress of public demands and appearances. It is the essential means of restoration and of learning the self. It can unexpectedly throw one into bitter loneliness, and married women with the responsibilities of home and children envy solitude—time to themselves often without acknowledging its dark side. Solitude comes with its price, but for Sarton it remains "a fabulous gift from the gods" (*JS*, 109). For Sarton, "solitude" has been a long love affair, has deepened as years have passed. She sees solitude as the sustaining force of her creative work, and above all, as she writes in *The House by the Sea* it is one way to learn how one is to grow old and to face death.

Evidence that her work reaches and touches people manifests itself in the countless letters that arrive daily. Over these, Sarton simultaneously exults and despairs, finding it essential to have this tangible proof of recognition, yet feeling intruded upon and doomed by the press of letters from fans. Ignoring advice to the contrary, she has persisted in this time-consuming labor of answering fan mail until the recent stroke forced her to abandon piles of letters, answering only those from friends long established. The unanswered letters verify her widespread appeal. People read her books and literally hundreds feel compelled to write. In spite of the burden the letters have caused, Sarton views them with gratitude, as proof that the work is getting out, being read, affecting people's lives. These letters testify always "what burdens people carry, how hard any life is at best—any life where there is caring and sensitivity—and the need to reach out" (*S*, 159).

The journal pages document the daily frustrations and irritations and they also document the order Sarton imposes so that a lifetime of writing has gone forward. She has usually shied away from her fellow writers, "partly because writing as a trade, is so competitive, and I am a bad loser. Any meeting with a successful writer opens wounds" (*S*, 55). Bound by honesty in the journals, Sarton confesses jealousy about writers who have won success, she exposes the details of her temper, rages, outbursts; she readily admits flaws in her own work while still smarting from unenthusiastic reviews when they come. She has chosen the metaphor herself that does encompass much of her life: like a villager of the Sherpas in Eastern Nepal who reads aloud the letter announcing that his wife has left him for another man, Sarton tells the unlovely, the humiliating (*R*, 246). To succeed as artist, she has had to expose far more of her private self than one expects or even, on occasion, wants. But she sees the private self bound intimately into the work, each destined to enrich and reflect the other, each destined to be put on paper.

The journals have allowed Sarton a forum for her political views that have from her youth been liberal. From her volunteer ambulance training during World War II to her daily responses to the television evening news, she has shown a keen and humane response to suffering, a keen intellectual response to political issues of our time. Calling herself always a political person, Sarton frequently centers on the holocaust as the epitome of terror and atrocity, seeing in that nightmare the absolute dark side of humankind. Her admiration has always gone to those capable at once of leadership and sacrifice, her sympathy to those who endure physical and political suffering that is not likely to change within their lifetime. Her impatience with current political leadership in America is particularly sharp in *At Seventy:* "Reagan's greatest failure is that he never appeals to the best in us, never asks sacrifice that would be meaningful to the common man, never lifts the spirit. What a mean-spirited, dreadful time this is in our country!" (*S,* 255).

Particularly in the last three journals, Sarton distills the experiences of pain, solitude, and death in passages that will strike readers as firmly as lines of poetry. It is such passages that have drawn readers to identify with the experiences, for in these passages Sarton sustains her vision, her perception of truth. "Pain is the great teacher. . . . And, curiously enough, pain draws us to other human beings in a significant way, whereas joy or unhappiness to some extent, isolates" (*R,* 208). Sarton writes about the fatal illness that beset her old friend in Nelson, Mildred Quigley: "I can only pray that she goes now in peace, that she does not have to make the huge effort to recover" (*S,* 273). And she reflects upon death: "But it is only when one is dying, like Laura in *A Reckoning,* that one is allowed to shut life out and concentrate on 'the real connections'" (*R,* 48). On the death of Judith Matlack who had been ravaged by illness, Sarton says, "I have prayed that she might be allowed to slip away, and now she has. But it is always so sudden, so unexpected—death—so final" (*S,* 213). And as I have noted, Sarton has had to face her own mortality in the illness brought on by the stroke, that sensation that "is too complex, too terrible, too astonishing and so the wave of memory dashes itself against rocks" (manuscript of *After the Stroke,* 1).

A journal is a record of a person's life—not only for the actual time the pages cover, but for the past that impinges upon the present and for the future that grows from both. The good journal writer tells the truth, the reader assumes, and in turn the reader accepts the life as lived and reported. There is, of course, in autobiographical writing what Sarton calls some sleight of hand going on. To avoid hurting, embarrassing, dismaying others, the writer must omit some things, give some people anonymity. Referring to people by initials (X, etc., in *Recovering* and in *Journal of Solitude*) provides anonymity but irritates the reader. Most of all in Sarton's journals the strength lies in her forthrightness as a person and in her skill as a writer. She is especially effective in descriptive passages of the garden, the sea, animals, light, as well as in rendering vivid accounts of events in her life. She has literally shared her deepest experiences with the reader. She has demonstrated the rich, full lives of women who never married, and she has willingly given herself away in these journals.

Early in *Journal of a Solitude* Sarton catalogs the writers she cherishes: Traherne, Herbert, Simone Weil, Turgenev, Trollope, Henry James, Virginia Woolf, E. M. Forster. She sees them collectively as modest, private, self-actualizers, writers outside the mainstream of their era. They function, Sarton contends, as "the moderate human voice, what might be called 'the human milieu,'—this is supremely unfashionable and appears to be irrelevant. But there always have been and always will be people who can breathe only there and who are starved for nourishment. I am one of those readers and I am also one who can occasionally provide the food" (*JS,* 67–68). Hundreds of readers would agree that she has so provided, and in abundance.

Finally, the journals record a balance often thinly held and present a remarkably frank account of a difficult, fragile, and fascinating personality. Sarton has followed her own advice: "Keep busy with survival. Imitate the trees. Learn to lose in order to recover, and remember that nothing stays the same for long, not even pain, psychic pain. Sit it out. Let it all pass. Let it go" (*JS,* 34). Because she has written these journals, Sarton has made it possible for herself and for many of her readers "to keep busy with survival."

## Chapter Three

# "I Shall Write Volumes": Sarton's Novels

The appearance of May Sarton's first book of poems in 1936 marked decisively her turn from active and immediate theater performance and directing to the more private and passive life of a poet. In 1938 she published her first novel (the most poetic of them all) and began a group of novels that number—if one counts the books for children and the fables—twenty-one, a formidable effort. That first novel, *The Single Hound,* derives its title from lines of Emily Dickinson that set forth themes emerging throughout Sarton's fiction.

> Adventure most unto itself
> The Soul condemned to be—
> attended by a single hound—
> Its own identity.[1]

Sarton's characters, by and large, are not travelers or adventurers; when they do travel, their journeys are usually routine or at least not journeys of great distances or startling adventures. Rather, they are journeys that inevitably lead the character (generally a woman) to find her own identity. There are, of course, some real geographic journeys, but changes of scene may not have significant consequences. For instance, Jane Reid in *The Magnificent Spinster* goes from Boston to Germany and stays for three years embroiled in the relief work that followed World War II. Her experience, however, strikes the reader as evidence of her lifelong political involvement. The experience does not change her as a person nor even substantially enrich her except as it reaffirms her instinct for justice.

The primary concern in Sarton's novels is the full discovery of the self, an action that touches many characters, an action that involves far more women characters than men. Sarton herself insists that she hopes her work shows the whole human—the whole human with all strengths and weaknesses, with the potential for change, with the will to lead life as the basic self dictates.

In her study of *Kinds of Love, As We Are Now,* and *Crucial Conversations* Gayle Gaskill draws inferences that are true for all of Sarton's work. In looking at Sarton's redefinition of traditional Christian emblems and outlooks, Gaskill suggests that Sarton and some of her primary characters perceive "a widening gap between Christian virtue and public morality." This discovery derives from an idealistic and humanistic outlook. Furthermore, characters who are not drawn or led to this stage easily engage in "action without ethics." As Sarton's focal characters face serious difficulties—middle age, solitude, divorce, old age, dying—they are led to "thoughtful self-study, thoughtful examinations of personal moral growth."[2] Throughout Sarton's work, readers can, if they will, be led to a deeper awareness of the obvious facts that wisdom does come through suffering, that average and ordinary people must face the extremes of solitude and old age, that an enriched and discovered self cannot emerge without meditation, solitude, self-examination, suffering, change. That these extremes often go undetected by other characters is true. Indeed, to depict internal growth and awareness and to bring women characters to a first realization of themselves as selves does not always result in fiction of primarily overt action. Instead, what results is often internal debate and agony that then must lead—as Sarton entitles one of her novels—to crucial conversations.

A traditional view, of course, assumes that women can (and should) find themselves and their fulfillment in life through marriage and motherhood like Kate Chopin's Adele Ratignolle, that woman-mother and sensuous madonna, as Chopin describes her. Although Sarton presents married couples at various ages and in various financial and social conditions, she never sentimentalizes marriage. And none of her women characters find the life-style represented in Adele Ratignolle acceptable for them.

To Willa Cather, marriage seemed to be—certainly in several novels—a negative state that a woman chose because she could not succeed as an artist or thrive in business. Marriage relegated women to inferior roles at best. Mrs. Harling in *My Ántonia* for example, is a vivacious and central figure until her husband returns to the house. Then her entire attention (and that of the household as well) must be turned to his demanding ways. Noise and individual concerns cease while he is

served. Late in the novel, we see Ántonia proud of the land she has
tilled and the children she has borne. But Cather uses the title "Cu-
zack's Boys" when she writes of Ántonia's married life, a title that
slights the mother and the daughters. Further, Ántonia is now forty-
five, and her *self* is absorbed totally into farm and family. Indeed, she
is physically spent—a woman nearly toothless, a vital farm woman,
but worn lean.

Sarton's view of marriage resembles Cather's, and often a harsh view
of marriage dominates. In Sarton's novels married women usually have
lost their sense of themselves and even when they move into careers
and succeed, men seldom acknowledge them or take them fully into
account. The range of marriage experiences is wide and very few of
Sarton's novels fail to deal with the issue. In her first extended treatment of marriage and family life, *The Bridge of Years* (1946), Sarton
takes the Duchesne family through the suffering of post–World War I
up to the onset of World War II.

In part, the novel is about an Edenic country house and about an
interesting, complicated marriage. The wife is magnetic, resourceful,
and competent without having intellectual brilliance. Her talent for
design and for business are talents inherited from her mother, talents
that allow her to assume a role reversal: she leaves the house each day
for the city and work while her husband, a failed philosopher, stays at
home with his migraines and his arid intellectual life—a nonworking/
earning husband. Even though he accepts his wife's earning power, he
gives up none of his own demands. The household must be quiet and
orderly, be run to meet his schedule and to suit his needs. In the beginning it had been the marriage of a talented woman to a handsome
man—so handsome a man that apparently no woman could resist him.
His early publishing effort is a five-year struggle to produce a philo-
sophical treatise that impresses no one. Through it all, the wife, Melanie, continues to adore him.

As the working woman, Melanie takes up the burdens of the breadwinner. "From far off they saw her striding along, swinging her brief-
case. . . . Everyday Melanie felt she was just holding off bankruptcy
by a miracle."[3] It is she, not the husband, who demands to know
Jacques's intentions toward the maid Lou-Lou, which, in fact, are to
flirt, not to marry. The great wound of Melanie's early married years
was Paul's refusal to father children after their first child was born.
Only in the euphoria of finishing his book is Paul willing to let his
family grow larger. But the growth of his family does not offset the

bitterness he embraces when the book fails. As the years pass, Melanie keeps their old friends and makes new ones; Paul has virtually no friends now because "he had gradually withdrawn from them or alienated them with his *'esprit critique'*" (16). His childish and irritable nature quickly spoils even a pleasant family dinner hour. Without warning he will blurt out, "'The soup is cold.' . . . He was as unpredictable as a summer sky" (29).

Paul's emotional immaturity and his professional failure are somewhat offset by his growing acceptance—in middle age—of life and failure. He finally accompanies his wife to the business each day, takes an interest, exerts some energy. And it is through him that the most profound insights in the novel come. When their employee, Mlle Louvais, confesses to Paul that her lover has abandoned her for a younger woman, Paul's response reflects sensitively upon the human condition. "Old old story, Paul thought. And yet it was not like that. Because at the bottom of it was the helpless, devouring need to love, to love through everything and in spite of everything, beyond humiliation, beyond despair. Only children and the very old know this love, understand it, love naked without hope, without anything to sustain it, without anything to help it through the bad times as marriage does, as physical passion does" (110–11).

Because Paul has a wife and three beautiful daughters, Mlle Louvais assumes that he enjoys "his whole natural life"—that is, a happy and fruitful marriage. Thus he could not understand her plight, her abandoned self, her being utterly unattached and "shut away from all normal joys and sorrows" (112), could not even know what she was talking about. Paul's response to her outburst is chilling, true, confessional; it touches an undeniable truth about life, a truth Sarton conveys sharply in this novel, and she insists it is a truth all should face. "Look into people's lives," Paul says, "Look into anyone's life. There is always a nightmare somewhere. . . . I am nothing, a poor father, a poor husband—yes I am inconsiderate, selfish—and a bad philosopher" (113). The happy appearance, the placid public appearance exist; so does the nightmare.

Late in the novel, with Melanie and Paul well into middle age, Sarton shows that love can be reestablished, that a marriage strained for years by tensions threatening its dissolution can be realigned and taken up again. This renewal of a fractured marriage is a theme fully carried out in *Kinds of Love,* but in *The Bridge of Years* the promise of renewal is overshadowed by the imminent approach of World War II.

It is 1940 and in Europe "the greens had never looked so brilliant. . . . It was like Eden before the fall. . . . Well it had come. For nearly ten years it had been on the way . . . in a few hours, in a day, the atmosphere changed to panic" (333–37).

The dark days of war dominate the latter part of the novel, but the idea of failed marriage has been a major theme throughout. The talented women in the novel succeed through their business and artistic selves, not through fulfillment in love and marriage. "One can," Melanie declares to her friend Simone, "get lost, far away from each other, even in a real marriage" (169). Those women who are found, find themselves; part of the price usually is the dissolution of the marriage—through divorce, through uncontrollable and external events (like the war), or through the husband's debilitation or death. That is to say, for women it is virtually impossible to have it all—to have a happy marriage and a successful artistic or professional life. Only the most exceptional, only the rare can have both. Marriage for most women has to mean playing Mrs. Ramsey: she must bring endless harmony out of endless chaos. The complex marriages in Sarton's work take into account the woman. She may once have loved her husband passionately, she may still "be in love," or she may have fallen out of love. On occasion, it is the man who suffers from the marriage more than the woman does. Whatever the state, Sarton consistently suggests that marriage has kept the woman's full self from emerging.

The marriages may also involve the children, who, if they are small, are often the usual reason that the parents stay together; if the children are older, they resent the divorce and usually take sides. In several of Sarton's novels, particularly *Shadow of a Man* and *Anger,* willful and selfish mothers have so maimed their sons that a happy marriage is difficult, especially when the son's wife is strong, independent, talented. Still another complication in marriage is "the other woman" who has her role in several of Sarton's novels, but never is she more than a threat. In *The Bridge of Years* everybody knows that Mlle Louvais has for years been a kept woman when Paul begins every day to spend hours with her. Melanie makes no protest, undertakes no intervention. She simply says, "He's not in love with her—at least I don't think so" (170). In *A Shower of Summer Days* fifty-year-old Violet (still incomparably beautiful) is perfectly aware of Charles's affairs, but is not threatened by them. "She had never cared before about the other women. . . . He did it cleanly and well . . . knowing always that the tide would eventually turn back to her and quite willing to accept a double standard."[4] The exception comes when the other woman may be Violet's summer charge, her own young niece. But this brief flirtation of Charles and young Sally remains nothing more than a flirtation.

What makes Sarton's treatment of marriage distinct is the persistent theme of friendship between women, not simply the marriages that are portrayed in much of their complexity. Often the wife will have a woman friend—sometimes one who goes all the way back to childhood—to whom she can talk. That in itself is not an exceptional occurrence in life or in fiction, but Sarton emphasizes the extreme importance of the friendship, which is almost always passionate. An overt or, more usually a sublimated, lesbian relationship, is often present: Hilary and Willa (*Mrs. Stevens Hears the Mermaids Singing*), Melanie and Simone (*The Bridge of Years*), Laura and Ella (*A Reckoning*), Persis and Solange (*Shadow of a Man*), to name but four examples. In interviews Sarton has commented on the friendship between women, declaring from her point of view that the passionate friendship and adoration of woman for another woman was, to Europeans, not aberrant or shocking but simply part of growth. Speaking of her mother's generation, she says that these passionate friendships were there, whether they ever became sexual or not. What must be stressed and what deserves serious consideration is this whole theme: the deep friendship between women that brings forth a level of communication and a sense of communion that is absent from the other parts of a woman's life. For instance, in *The Birth of a Grandfather* two women characters respond to each other at the deepest level possible. "When she and Lucy were together, Frances *thought aloud,* and thought things she would not have come upon otherwise, or admitted she had" (my italics).[5]

The level of communication achieved when one can think aloud is the point—not whether the relationship between the women is a sexual one or not. Without question, the driving force in May Sarton's life and work centers in the word *communion*—that sense of perfect wholeness and harmony so difficult for humans to achieve. That communion is, of course, possible in marriage and indeed falsely assumed to accompany all marriages. But Sarton finds that the deepest communion comes between two women, and the theme appears in novel after novel, always taking into account the individual character and need of the particular woman. This deep friendship between women is primary, and the issue is not stereotyped and never simple. It is, however, the focal point for the women as they discover who they are, as they face limitations and growth, as they respond to this real presence of friendship.

These women are friends, they are loving friends, and for most of them this relationship extends over a lifetime and is so much a part of their existence that they hardly recognize how much of life has been influenced by the friendship and how much of their lives depend upon it. For Christina and Ellen (*Kinds of Love*), the friendship has lasted for sixty years, strained by their radically different economic status and sustained by "the quality of silence between them that had made this friendship last and renew itself over all the years."[6] Quite often, this friendship between two women is a far deeper experience than the conventional marriage has been for them. In a piece in the *New York Times Book Review*, "That Certain Thing Called the Girlfriend," Margaret Atwood claims that "despite their late blooming, women's friendships are now firmly on the literary map as valid and multidimensional novelistic material."[7] In novel after novel May Sarton explores the dimensions and the depth of that material.

## The Myth of the Happy Marriage

To reach this real sense of their real selves, Sarton's women characters write in journals (Christina in *Kinds of Love*, Caro in *As We Are Now*), meditate seriously upon the meaning of past action (Hilary in *Mrs. Stevens Hears the Mermaids Singing*, Laura in *A Reckoning*), confront the impossible direction their lives have taken (Poppy in *Crucial Conversations*, Joanna in *Joanna and Ulysses*), reconcile themselves to the restrictions of old age (Jane Tuttle in *Kinds of Love*, Doro in *The Single Hound*, Aunt Minna in *A Reckoning*). Many of these women struggle to find identity because they are confined in the web of married life.

Over and over again the myth of the happy marriage is played out as the unmarried family friend in *Crucial Conversations* well knows. Phillip watches as Poppy and Reid's marriage disintegrates and thinks, "Marriage has always seemed to me one of those impossibilities that men work at in the wild hope that this one, theirs, is going to prove that the impossible can be achieved."[8] The wife who wants to be more than wife is an old, old theme. Ibsen's Nora wants to be more than a doll in a doll's house; when Kate Chopin's Edna wants to become a painter, her husband Leonce refuses to let an affinity for art interrupt her duties in maintaining the household routine. In *Crucial Conversa-*

*tions* Poppy wants to be a sculptor free of a twenty-six-year marriage, wants to find out if her work can be art, not therapy.

In *Anger* Hilda, the wife of Paul Fraser, has ceased fighting her husband's acid manner. She has begun to paint and to paint seriously. When Anna asks if Paul minds Hilda's preoccupation with painting, she replies, "Oh, I expect so. . . . We never talk about it. He isn't interested . . . and maybe that's just as well."[9] In *Faithful Are the Wounds* Sarton sets a brief part of the plot in a slightly exotic California, drawing from the impressions she absorbed on visits there. *Faithful Are the Wounds,* one of her best works, is based primarily on the Cambridge, Massachusetts, scene and in particular bases the protagonist, Edward Cavan, on F. O. Matthiessen, a distinguished Harvard professor, who committed suicide in 1950. The subplot of Edward Cavan's sister portrays a married life. Isabel's pride and identity center in her married name (Mrs. Henry Thomas Ferrier), in the fact that her husband is a prominent surgeon, and in her twenty-year marriage—the kind praised in *Good Housekeeping.* She has reared her children, pampered her husband, played endless games of backgammon in the evenings, and handled her own nameless despair by exerting unusual care in cooking, dressing fashionably, housekeeping. Until she is called upon to act when her brother commits suicide, her single gesture toward independence had been redecorating her living room. In this endeavor (not in running a business or in attempting to create art) "she had emerged into her real life, trusting her own judgment at last."[10]

Isabel's effort should not be dismissed as trivial, Sarton would argue. After all, her expectations in life had not included independence. Growing up, Isabel watched Edward (beloved of their mother) break through—having a year of study abroad, earning the Ph.D., securing a professorship. She had not broken through, she declares, because she "didn't have any way" (14). Although Sarton lets life in the Northeast reflect greater intellectual activity than Isabel's California world, the fate of married women throughout the novel is grim. In Julia Phillips (the wife of Edward's colleague, Damon) Sarton represents many wives of professional men. Damon (who will finally act with principle and conviction) is the brilliant, absentminded professor who assumes unceasing support from his wife. Again, the woman plays her role as nurturer: Damon never hears a word Julia says and "her job was to listen and to say appropriate things" (83). In her, we do explore the myth of the happy marriage. Julia still has the carriage and detail of her youth's great beauty, but her life teeters in a delicate balance: the outward appearance of the perfect wife, the inward longing to be her-self. "She had lifted him [Damon] again and again, patiently, quietly, and with what she imagined was love, but it had seemed to her for some time now that *she was acting a part, the part of the perfect wife.* Lately, she had felt a wild desire, to escape, to run away, to find out at long last what she herself was like, to live her own life, though she was very vague as to what this might be" (79, my italics).

As the novel progresses, her chances to really "live her own life" do not emerge and her view of marriage is, from the woman's point of view, an image of complete powerlessness. "Whatever we are, we are together. . . . When you marry someone you become a kind of Siamese twin—a woman does anyway" (226). The image says that the woman-in-marriage-as-Siamese-twin must take her signals from the male half or—at the very least—always support the male half so that a semblance of harmony exists. Julia concludes that for woman, the role forever is that of the giver, the nurturer, the bringer of harmony, the accepting half of the married pair. "Strange," she ruminates, "how quickly it happened, the change—we are this warmth and this coldness, strangers, lovers, friends, enemies. People talk about 'a happy mar-riage' and it meant, she supposed, all this, the complex creation hour by hour and minute by minute, the revolt and the acceptance. And now the meal ready, arrival at the end of the day" (86). It is a candid look at what a marriage must be with all of its paradoxes, and the scene ends with the woman in her role providing the evening meal.

The exploration of the marriage theme continues in *Kinds of Love,* in which Christina Chapman resents her husband's considering her talent as a painter to be merely a pleasant diversion, like his court tennis: "To take it seriously, to be a professional, would have been not done, would have meant losing one's amateur status" (26). Christina's resentment has lasted fifty years; now in her seventies, she still feels deprived. There is no evidence in *Kinds of Love* or in *Crucial Conversations* that Christina or Poppy would have succeeded as artists. Chances are, they would not. But they both have been denied the chance, denied the experience that could for better or worse have changed them, made new demands, brought forth more of their essential selves. It is too late now for Christina to try, but Poppy is divorcing to enter a new life that *will* change her, if only by letting her fail.

Sarton's women characters are not all hopeful artists, but their mar-riages are still portrayed as life-styles that deny them independence and development. One of the most vivid indictments comes in *The Birth of a Grandfather* where an array of marriage problems appear. The main characters, Frances and Sprig Weyth, have what appears to be a happy marriage but are, as the husband says, "as distant from each other as two stars" (5). Within this marriage the wife's role is clearly defined: "her job was to sustain, to center, to be everyone's security and comfort" (6). It is a marriage that finally brings forth rage as Frances "suddenly hated his closed face, even his teasing smile, his rejection of her, his making her into a sewer on of buttons" (193).

The relegation of women to secondary roles is epitomized in Sprig's reaction to the news that their friends, John and Lucy, are divorcing: "She forgets to send his shirts to the laundry" (28), absurdly implying that this act is a cause for divorce. The fact remains that if woman's primary role is to be everybody's security and daily comfort, she must then attend to the laundry as well as the buttons. Sarton does not by any means make her women characters flawless, artistically or personally. Poppy is middle-aged and stout, Lucy is a messy housekeeper (newspapers are all over the floor and the laundry is neglected), and Frances irritates when she constantly sips tea so loudly. The shortcomings are real, but they are hardly commensurate to the neglect these women suffer because of them and suffer for the larger issue—their refusing to be the stereotypic wife.

Even in *The Single Hound,* written when she was twenty-six, Sarton emphasizes women's disappointment in marriage: "Dozens of women come to Doro's house, bearing in their hands their manuscript poems—coming because they are unhappily married, because at thirty they had become terrified at the emptiness of their lives."[11] Their need for fulfillment is great but the fact remains that talent must be inherent before young women (or middle-aged women) can turn successfully to poetry and there make their lives. To be thoroughly disillusioned with marriage at thirty suggests how tentative that arrangement for life turns out, in reality, to be. The deep need for expression must be taken seriously, but the need no way guarantees that the expression will be worthy of the word poetry. The desire to be an artist does not make an artist.

*Anger* (1982) brings the preoccupation with marriage into a different milieu, but this novel also exposes the myth of the happy marriage. Here the wife Anna, an accomplished mezzo-soprano, is poised on the brink of a brilliant career. She marries a Boston banker, Ned Fraser, who is passionately devoted to music. Unlike Poppy and Christina, Anna is a fine artist, not just a hopeful one; her devotion to art is unwavering and her temper volatile. As the title implies, the novel is a study of anger and, within this marriage, anger constantly threatens.

At first, the marriage of Anna Lindstrom and Ned Fraser appears ideal. The matchmaker is a typical Sarton character type—a shrewd, old, independent woman. Ernesta Aldrich was exactly right in assuming the two would fall in love, but she could not know that their temperaments would clash so severely. The marriage is threatened not only by Anna's anger, but also by Ned's suppressing emotion and finding her angry outbursts unacceptable, inexcusable. Ned is like several other male characters in Sarton's work—a young man haunted by his father's early and tragic death and dominated by his mother, a severe, selfish, demanding woman.

Ned and Anna are attractive and indeed physically drawn to each other. (The novel contains by far Sarton's most explicit sexual scenes.) But the marriage threatens to stifle the wife's career and upset the husband's psychological state. Uncontrolled anger is simply the obvious problem. Anna regrets but cannot forestall the outbursts that Ned finds intolerable. At the end of the novel they are still married: Ned has come to a deeper understanding about his father's death (it was not an accident but a suicide of despair), and Anna realizes that while her attacks of anger do lead to communication—she does get Ned's attention—the outbursts also carry within them destructive elements. While neither the husband nor the wife is blameless, Sarton favors Anna whose costly outbursts echo Sarton's unwavering view that people should let feelings out, should honor their feelings. Anger, Sarton has said frequently, has a great deal to teach, if a person will let it.

Unlike many of the other women characters struggling against marriage to find themselves, Anna is not middle-aged, stout, or untalented. To the outsider, the marriage of Ned and Anna is perfect. Both are handsome, successful, surrounded by luxury: they have what others envy. Their marriage, however, is far from a storybook romance. In the 1974 introduction for the reissue of *Mrs. Stevens Hears the Mermaids Singing* Carolyn Heilbrun argues that "if Sarton seems to bow too low to the convention of the proper wifely functions, she does know that the real artist is not the fantasy creature imagined by women trapped in domesticity." Indeed, Sarton has no such illusion and shares with Heilbrun the understanding that "the real artist is engaged in a full-time struggle, which is harder for women, among other reasons, because they do not have wives."[12]

The struggle in *Anger* is the struggle of the nearly impossible—the struggle of a woman to be artist and wife. Although the novel does not end with the divorce of Ned and Anna, neither does it end with a resolution of their marital problems. Both gain understanding of their own demons and of the other's difficulty. But the marriage, if it does continue, will not be an easy one and it is important to emphasize this realistic ending. The myth of the happy marriage invites a "live happily ever after" for these two attractive people, especially when one remembers the severe conflicts they have at least confronted during the course of the novel. But Sarton ends the novel realistically, without sentimentality. The problems are deep and the pair has not solved them all.

Many women readers of *Anger* feel affinity with Anna. These women readers have risked outbursts of anger only, like Anna, to have husbands indifferent to or outraged by their cries. Women do not provide comfort and security when they vent anger. About midway through *Anger* Anna's mother (a woman whose surgeon husband thwarted but did not blight her life) sees the marriage dilemma as a power struggle. "It has always puzzled me . . . why people fall in love with people so unlike themselves and then apparently can't be satisfied or happy till they have tried to change the other into a likeness of themselves" (106). She herself had sublimated or forfeited her desire to change her husband and had lived as the wife he expected her to be.

In Anna, Sarton has a character whose sense of self and whose dedication to art would never let her be trapped by domesticity or be controlled by her husband. Other women go about life differently. Bewildered and wearied by Anna's angry outbursts, Ned finally asks his mother if she and his father ever had angry, violent scenes.

"Anger?" she had said, raising an eyebrow, "What a thing to imagine!"
"You were never cross with him?"
"If I was, I didn't show it," she said, and as he waited in silence, she built her defenses. "Of course, Ned, times have changed. When I was married the unbuttoned behavior of today would have been impossible—that was for the immigrants, not for us." (78)

The response of this woman's generation and class was very real. The next generation of women—if they are like Anna—will not react in such a way. And to be angry, to express anger openly, is hardly a feminine attribute that society applauds or condones. The nineteenth-century clergyman's warning to women is still alive: "Stay within your proper confines, and you will be worshipped; . . . step outside, and you will cease to exist."[13] Many of Sarton's women characters do, to a great extent, stay within the safe confines. Even while Melanie earns the family living, she continues to be the wife who creates security and provides comfort, still acts as if the husband's work is more important than her own. Laura in *A Reckoning* becomes a skillful editor only after her children are grown and away from home, as if her career merely fills a void when it could have been her lifelong endeavor. The two women friends in *Kinds of Love* have suffered long marriages—Christina enclosed in a wealthy marriage, Ellen held in a marginal marriage of bone-chilling work and a driven husband. Both women have been denied real developing of themselves outside the demands of the marriage.

Many of Sarton's women characters are married, but none are fooled by the myth of the happy marriage. What is required of them is exactly what has always been required of married women: to provide security and comfort. The scene that ends chapter 6 in "The Window" portion of Virginia Woolf's *To the Lighthouse* shows Mrs. Ramsey forced to compose herself from a moment of severe irritation. She must restore order and she resumes knitting the stocking for the lame boy at the lighthouse. In doing so she diverts and settles her son James: "Knitting her reddish-brown hairy stocking, with her head outlined absurdly by the gilt frame, the green shawl which she had tossed over the edge of the frame. . . . Mrs. Ramsey smoothed out what had been harsh in her manner a moment before, raised his head, and kissed her little boy on the forehead. 'Let us find another picture to cut out,' she said."[14]

In Sarton's latest novel, *The Magnificent Spinster (1985),* Cam (the narrator) speaks out of late middle age about her friend Faith, who has been married for many years: "she was leading a life I might have led as I was leading a life she might have led. . . . I don't wonder that she envied me at times, perhaps felt in a strange way muffled, swamped in family life. But did she understand that I too felt muffled in a university life."[15] Most of her unmarried women characters do not regret missing marriage, do not feel deprived because they have remained single. They lead rich lives, but they also live complicated lives. Just because the single woman does not have to answer to husband and children and their demands, their lives like Cam's can be muffled. However, their chances of discovering themselves and even of becoming artists are greater because, unlike wives and mothers, single women do not have domestic responsibilities as their primary concern.

## Sarton's Old Ladies

One particularly successful character that Sarton often portrays is the very old woman. She usually is eccentric, attracts younger friends (mostly men), maintains her independence, is politically active and liberal, does not fear the advance of age or the coming on of death. There are the three women teachers in *The Single Hound* who have made many compromises in life but who live fully their quiet existence. Doro (based on Sarton's Belgian teacher Marie Closset) at twenty had "looked like a frail boy with eyes too big for him," had loved Claudette (who chose to marry), and "Doro was left to get through the Belgian winter" (11) and had grown old. As teacher and as poet, she has been vigorous and independent. Jane Tuttle, ninety, may be infirm and now dependent on the inelegant housekeeper Hannah, but her influence still radiates. Her affinity with nature sustained her throughout a lifetime, and it is to her and to her instinctive sensitivity that the troubled characters in the novel can and do respond.

Aunt Jane in *The Birth of a Grandfather* is also ninety and the still point in a turbulent family primarily because she has never tried to reform herself or anybody else. Grace Kinnoch, the grand old lady in *Faithful Are the Wounds,* is politically engaged and constantly seeks battle. Edward Cavan is drawn to her, and together they oppose the encroachments upon the local academic and political scene that grow out of McCarthyism. Like Jane Tuttle and Jane Weyth, Grace Kinnoch is single and as deeply as any Sarton character faces her aloneness. "Our real lives are secret, she thought, frightfully secret. No one knows anyone else. Friendship, even love, fails. We are alone" (48). Like her servant Ellen, Grace is tall, thin, ageless—an old lady who rebounds again and again to speak up and to demand reason and justice from those inclined to ignore these virtues. Grace's friendship with the much younger Edward Cavan has established a real connection, one Sarton has echoed in other novels. Doro and Mark (*The Single Hound*), Hilary and Mar (*Mrs. Stevens Hears the Mermaids Singing*), Ellen and Joel, Jane Tuttle and John (*Kinds of Love*), all portray much older women, strong and, except for Ellen, liberated from domestic life as their primary responsibility. All play vital roles in the lives of young men; most of them also serve as foils to the mothers who have not fully responded to the needs of these sons. For the most part, these women are the odd one in a solid, conservative (and usually wealthy) family. While they may be mavericks, their zest for life and their genius for friendship give them full-bodied freshness and, to use Sarton's phrase, an expectant innocence.

They intuitively assist the vulnerable and simultaneously uphold their own commitments. For other characters, these older women represent a powerful link since they alone knew the younger characters as children. These women remember when all the others were young, were the innocent children these experienced adults now are. Even when the old woman is not alive during the action of the novel, her influence is considerable. The elderly Caro Spenser in *As We Are Now*, doomed to the despair of an improperly run nursing home, frequently remembers the strength of her long-dead Aunt Isabel. A Ph.D. in political science, Isabel drank and smoked with zest when "ladies" indulged in neither habit, and she had been Caro's older relative, her mentor. Isabel had even approved of the liaison between Caro and Alex, going to Paris to see for herself that they were—whatever the circumstances—properly matched. Out of the depths of her own old age and despair Caro remembers this older woman of her youth, a model to Caro then, and draws comfort from the memory even now. The ultimate memory of Aunt Isabel surfaces when Caro remembers that woman's strength and declares that had Isabel been alive, she (Caro) would not have been doomed to the care of an ill-run nursing home. "The truth is," Caro reminds herself, "that the people who could save the old in places like this have died—that is why we are put here, because there *is* no one."[16]

Three other examples point to the diversity Sarton employs within these old women characters. In *A Reckoning* Laura Spelman at sixty-two is dying of lung cancer. Widowed, she turned to a late but fruitful career as an editor only to have success stopped cold by cancer. For Laura, Aunt Minna is the link to childhood. This very old relative lives alone and in her active life had supported the League of Nations, the League of Women Voters, the Viet Nam protest, and busing blacks. Now she faces the unnatural task of watching her niece—so much younger than she—die. Aunt Minna does what she can; as health and the weather permit, she comes to Laura and reads aloud. ("You and Trollope are my best medicine," Laura said. "Let's read."[17]) The very sound of Aunt Minna's voice evokes for Laura the whole of the past within the present moment.

An old Russian voice teacher coaches Anna Lindstrom (*Anger*). Mariana Protopova's utter devotion to music demands full attention from Anna whose domestic unhappiness has unbalanced her singing technique. Protopova demands attention to primary matters. A singer will breathe properly; when a voice lesson begins, all the other world is forgotten. Jane Reid, the "magnificent spinster" (modeled on Sarton's devoted teacher and friend, Anne Thorp), has, from her youth into her old age, drawn children and adults of both sexes into her circle of influence. She has used her immense wealth wisely, been guided by her liberal instincts, remained an interesting individual. Early in this novel the narrator declares that Jane Reid "was never virginal" (61). This somewhat surprising statement touches most of Sarton's single women and echoes a point that Heilbrun makes in her text, *Toward a Recognition of Androgyny,* a point that fits Sarton's characters. Heilbrun links Spenser's Britomart to a Greek concept of virginity: "For Spenser, chastity does not mean guarding of one's maidenhead but, at least insofar as Britomart is concerned, a complicated concept having to do with honorable love, reminding us of what virginity meant to certain Greeks: a state of autonomy and self-reliance, not sexual inexperience."[18] So it is for Sarton's older women characters. The reader is not so concerned about the presence or absence of love affairs in their pasts as she is struck by these women who manifest in their old age the autonomy and self-reliance they have nurtured throughout their lives. In our American world of advertisements praising youth and beauty Sarton's serious portrayal of old peole as vital, useful, and interesting makes a good gesture at balance.

It is important that Sarton's perceptive and sensitive portrayal of the old began when she herself was young. At twenty-six, she writes of Doro (*The Single Hound*) as she grows old, admits infirmities, faces death. The title of part 1, "Prelude. Time is a Dreaming," mirrors Doro's meditation on age and death, a meditation that Sarton writes with considerable empathy. "Was this," Doro says to herself, "getting old, this devouring sense of the past which looked so often blurred and then suddenly stood out distinct as if her eyes could only focus there" (41). As Doro suffers spells of vertigo, finds errands a chore, encounters difficulty in simply dressing and undressing, she has moments of suddenly feeling very old and being struck with the fear of dying—that inescapable reality. "I've been taming death ever since I can remember," she says (21).

In her own middle age Sarton wrote *Kinds of Love*. Here, Christina Chapman articulates that moment when a woman must admit that now she is the older generation. All those people of her youth are dead—those adults who knew her as a child—and she must take into account the obvious and the subtle reminders of age: nearly grown grandchildren, a husband severely crippled by a stroke, her arthritic knee that makes climbing steps a battle, her age of seventy-five. Christina confides in her journal that basic paradox: the aging flesh yet houses a youthful spirit: "Growing old is so strange because *inside* one feels just the same" (143). Sarton does portray old age and conveys the limits age imposes, but she also celebrates age and insists that we look forward to its possibilities.[19] It is not a time when feeling and even passionate flirtation, love, and jealousy are dead. She has called *Kinds of Love* a novel that is partly about love in old age, and in Christina Sarton portrays an ever-feminine woman who at seventy-five still experiences the flutter of deep feeling and desire.

## The Acceptance of Androgyny

The idea of androgyny threads its way throughout Sarton's novels, ranging from the simple dress of small children to more complex adult realization of masculine and feminine traits within one individual. Sarton views the whole person as one who recognizes and welcomes both traits within his or her being. Not all characters, however, can nurture both sides of the self. The stereotypic fear is part of *A Reckoning,* but a fear that threatens the husband, Brooks, not his wife or his mother. Laura Spelman listens as her daughter-in-law Ann describes her own two children:

"Laurie is a tremendously vital little girl. I must tell you something rather amusing," Ann interrupted herself. "Charley really wants to be a girl too, and he is very feminine, you know."

"And nobody is going to worry about that," Laura said. "Wonderful things are happening, Ann, and one, I think, don't you, is the acceptance of androgyny."

"Brooks worries." (100)

As a child, Jane Reid (*The Magnificent Spinster*) identified that part of her that would like to be a man—to become like Cyrano, "swash-buckling, in love with language, with an irresistible power to woo . . . but doomed to failure because of an immense nose" (61). Melanie (the wife, mother, breadwinner) looks back at her early years and wonders "if her dreams had not been a man's dreams—and even her young life of passionate free attachments to women, a young man's life" (*Bridge*, 187). Cam remembers in middle age the "unisex clothing" at Warren School where she went as a child. That manner of dress was welcomed, a great relief, since "sixty years ago, blue jeans for girls did not exist, and in most schools a girl was expected to look like a girl and wear dresses" (*Spinster*, 78).

In *Anger* Sarton explores a more complex realization of androgynous elements within an individual. Anna wonders if the masculine in her-self and in her husband Ned is not at war with the feminine in each of them. She attributes Ned's sensitivity to flowers, art, and music to his feminine side, a side he has apparently made peace with. She presumes that his masculine side makes him refuse to discuss any aspect of feel-ing, and she concludes that is why he can express tender feelings and words only to his dog. To further complicate their relationship, Ned dislikes and resents the feminine side of Anna—her need for tender words, her outbursts of tears. Yet when Anna lashes out in anger (a masculine trait), Ned considers her behavior aberrant. Women are not to vent anger. Ned's resistance to expressing his own feelings and his refusal to allow Anna hers bring the marriage to an impasse.

Androgyny in *A Shower of Summer Days* centers on a young woman named Sally whose mother objects to Ivan, the young man Sally thinks she loves. So, for the summer, Sally is abroad, living at Dene's Court with her mother's sister Violet and Charles, Violet's husband.[20] Sally's rebellion manifests itself in her messy room, loud music, and her clothes—"blue jeans too tight . . . with an absurd boy's checked shirt . . . androgynous, remote as a sulky schoolboy" (81). As it turns out, Ivan's visit proves him to be less than the ideal suitor and brings out Sally's resentment of typical feminine expectations. "Women," she la-ments, "have to wait around and see what men will do first. They can never act on their own" (197).

Superficially by dress and temperamentally by actions, Sally exhibits masculine traits; however, her feminine side draws her passionately to her aunt. (At the same time, Charles almost indulges in a serious summer affair with Sally.) The deep love Sally feels for Violet reveals a latent lesbian theme—a desire both women recognize. The awareness of woman's passionate love for woman comes to Sally as the silent love she holds for Violet, her wishing "to be enclosed accepted once and for all, to love and to be passionately loved by Violet" (133). For Violet it is a matter of recognition and feeling "quite miserable, in some way deprived because she was depriving, in some way starved because she could not feed Sally's passionate hunger. For the first time in her life, she faced the fact that a woman might long to give passionate love to another woman. It did not shock her" (144).

My point is not that androgynous traits must suggest lesbian traits; however, with the character Sally, her "masculine" dress and rebellious behavior are brought into focus by her passionate response to Violet. Charles, on the other hand, is flattered by the younger woman and, for a brief time, Sally becomes a rival when Violet sees the two embrace. Not realizing that Charles is simply comforting Sally, Violet misinterprets their embrace. Feeling the full weight of middle age (fifty-two), Violet now sees Sally not as a boyish girl but "as a real antagonist. It was a powerful collision" (114). In the end, Violet and Charles continue their life together. Sally sees that, at thirty, Ivan is hopelessly self-centered, and through Sally's growth Sarton conveys a primary theme: "By mastering feeling, she [Sally] had come to understand the meaning of discipline and its reward: freedom and power" (225).

Androgyny is present in a radically different novel, *The Small Room,* where the formidable Carryl Cope is given masculine traits almost entirely. She wears a crumpled seersucker suit and "elegant black slippers like a man's evening slippers; she speaks abruptly ("My name's Cope. Who are you!"); she swears in public and characteristically is demanding ("Damn nonsense" . . . "Hallie," . . . she cried imperiously, "where are you!"); and drinks tea and this novel's ever-present martinis "down in one gulp."[21] Lucy Winter, a newcomer to this small academic community, had expected Carryl Cope's appearance to match her formidable reputation—"to be huge . . . and she was quite small. She had expected her to be handsome, and saw instead a faded yellowish face, fine hair like a child's, cut short, no make-up at all, eyes that narrowed rather than opened so one could not name their color, and a very pointed nose" (17–18).

Carryl Cope's masculine gestures and the scholarly reputation reflect her professional success. Her stature, however, suggests traits more childlike than simply feminine—a physical appearance somewhat androgynous, and certainly lacking in traditional feminine charm. Yet a faculty wife, Maria Beveridge, is jealous, "black with jealousy of that old bluestocking. It is ridiculous" (224). Maria's words can be read two ways: it is ridiculous to be jealous because there is nothing in the relationship of Carryl Cope and Jack Beveridge to cause her jealousy or it is ridiculous to be jealous of a woman who is not beautiful. In the latter reading we are back again to an element of androgyny: if the masculine side is obvious, is ascendant, then the feminine side should be no threat to traditional relationships. The relationship in Carryl Cope's life has been her love for Olive Hunt throughout these years without having the courage to live openly with her. And the novel will see Carryl's spirit broken—first by her plagiarizing student and then by her sharp disagreement with Olive over the endowment she has named in her will for the college.

It is, of course, in *Mrs. Stevens Hears the Mermaids Singing* that Sarton best expresses the androgynous link to the homosexual side of characters. Hilary Stevens's father had declared he wanted a girl; Hilary herself had declared she "wanted to *be* a boy, I guess" (63). She was, at least, given an androgynous name. Certainly her passionate longings were not directed toward her husband during their brief marriage, but toward women—Phillippa Munn in her youth and her great love, Willa MacPherson. In her old age (seventy) Hilary deals with the young man named Mar whose brief homosexual encounters have left him deeply troubled. Hilary Stevens enters his life by chance. Now as his confidante, she listens to his despairing words, reads his unsuccessful poems, perceives his limitations and his possibilities. In him, Mrs. Stevens sees "a buried part of herself. Mar was the young man she had dreamed of being. . . . Turn that troubled, troubling face around and it was her own face" (214).

Here Sarton echoes her paradoxical poem "The Muse as Medusa" in *A Grain of Mustard Seed.* In the poem the speaker risks the fatal act: "I looked you straight in the cold eye, cold." The speaker is not turned to stone but is turned instead to inspiration, to poetry. "But I saw you, Medusa, made my wish / And when I left you I was clothed in thought." At the end of the poem the identification comes as the muse as Medusa and the speaker coalesce:

> I turn your face around! It is my face.
> That frozen rage is what I must explore—

> Oh secret, self-enclosed, and ravaged place!
> This is the gift I thank Medusa for.

The connection between Mar and the old lady exists on an artistic and on an emotional level. He is the young man Hilary Stevens might have been. Poetry and, to a lesser degree, homosexuality have drawn these two together. As a successful poet and as the older figure, Hilary does represent "masculine wisdom." As the sensitive figure, suffering from life, love, rejection, Mar is the weaker figure or, if you will, the "feminine."[22] More important, however, these two are part of each other: on one level, androgynous, coalescing the two natures to make one perfect whole. Hilary murmurs, "Everyone is everyone, . . . only you and I are more so" (214).

In her study, *Knowing Women: A Feminine Psychology,* Irene Claremont de Castillejo explains the male/female condition: "the basic masculine view is on focus, division, change; the feminine (in either sex) is more nearly an attitude of acceptance, an awareness of the unity of all life and a readiness for relationship." Such attitudes indeed account for a "rough division of the psyche into masculine and feminine." The sharp differences in sex roles and traits have somewhat given way, and de Castillejo suggests that "today, when masculine and feminine characteristics are so interwoven in people of both sexes, it may be clearer to speak of 'focused consciousness' on the one and 'diffuse awareness' on the other, knowing that these qualities belong to both men and women in varying degrees."[23] Sarton's characters may recognize androgyny, but accepting the idea is a different matter. The concepts of change and responsibility for change are central in Sarton's fiction. Often the character must accept the responsibility for reordering "his" world to give meaning to "her" life. When this reordering emphasizes the feminine within the masculine or the masculine within the feminine, that condition for a character is difficult. For a Ned Fraser, almost impossible. Yet such a balance is crucial. By considering Lytton Strachey's essay on Florence Nightingale, Carolyn Heilbrun drives home this point. "He [Strachey] at least understood that sweetness without intelligence and forcefulness is as powerless as masculine domination without the balance of femininity is destructive. In those who accomplish much, the elements are frequently so mixed that mankind might stand up and say: there is a human being."[24] Sarton's hope that her work, as a whole, can be seen as idealistic and humanistic requires the recognition and the acceptance of androgyny. For in that state one sees all of the self, one attains the balance (masculine and feminine, force and sweetness), one is a human being.

## The Problem of Woman as Woman and Artist

In 1974 W. W. Norton reissued *Mrs. Stevens Hears the Mermaids Singing* (1965) and its appearance marked a turning point in Sarton's career. A year earlier a special session at the annual meeting of the Modern Language Association was entitled "The Art of May Sarton." The ten papers were delivered by competent scholars, but scholars who for the most part did not enjoy wide national reputations. The appearance of *Mrs. Stevens* in 1974 with Carolyn G. Heilbrun's imprimatur was another matter. Heilbrun is a prominent scholar, a distinguished professor at Columbia University, an influential feminist critic (especially for her study, *Reinventing Womanhood*), a successful author of mystery novels (the Amanda Cross novels)—in short, a figure of national prominence. Thus Sarton and her work were introduced by a critic who is known (if not universally admired) by the established academic community. Now dissertations at major universities are being written on Sarton's work; her poems continue to be anthologized; her public readings have long been in demand from town halls in New England villages to the platforms of university auditoriums. There is a public of devoted readers and a growing body of scholars who value Sarton's work with critical objectivity.

*Mrs. Stevens* deserves attention because, among other reasons, it serves well to illustrate the strengths and the weaknesses in most of Sarton's novels. For all its strength, weaknesses exist: convoluted conversations, a tendency in characters toward overintrospection, a thinness of plot. Doris Grumbach made the point clearly when she reviewed *Crucial Conversations:* "We are still waiting for what we have always expected [Sarton] would some day do, and has not yet quite done. Her work gives us the sense of the perpetually promising; we look back over a just-read work with regret born of our recognition of her partial success."[23] The same can be said of *Mrs. Stevens:* however, one readily admits that this partial success is impressive. Grumbach's overall assessment is fair, especially so compared to John Gardner's review in the *Southern Review* where he calls Sarton "a careful craftsman with considerable skill," then diminishes the compliment by declaring that she is shallow. In *Mrs. Stevens* Gardner finds the internal conversations Hilary engages in "stagey," the names (Adrian and Mar)

"fussy," the characters basically "a brilliant cast of fops." Gardner ends
his brief review with a truism and dismisses Sarton all too casually:
"Great writing requires a great person to do the writing. Miss Sarton
leaves us with fine craftsmanship and a trivial view of man and—the
real subject of the novel—poetry."[26] *Mrs. Stevens* has flaws, but in this
novel Sarton's view of man and her treatment of poetry and the poet
are by no means trivial.

*Mrs. Stevens* is an interesting novel, centering on a concern many
writers share, a concern "with the life of the artist, and with the artistic
rendering of life" (Heilbrun introduction, xiii). Sarton's novel focuses
on Hilary Stevens, a poet who is now an old woman and lately come
to fame. Time and circumstance (a young couple arrives to interview
Hilary) set off a chain of remembered events. Hilary's flights into
memory suspend the novel's present action. As the interviewers pose
questions, Hilary drifts into memory, goes once to lie down, goes out
onto the terrace on another occasion. But the lifetime remembered
compensates for the technical problems. That life is indeed a rich one.
The reader finds a careful exploration of how one person has experienced life as woman and as artist. Sarton makes Hilary confront both
the limitations of her old age and of her life as artist. In retrospect, it
is a portrait of an artist, in particular of a woman artist. There are
distracting features: the novel falls into numbered parts and the divisions called "Interlude" and "Epilogue" are not experimental enough
to be inventive and distract from the narrative line. Hilary Stevens's
internal conversations at times become tedious. The names, however,
fit the characters that Sarton draws: Hilary, Mar, Adrian, Phillippa.
(Indeed Mar's name may reflect the youth's excursions with boating in
the novel. The sea image is also readily apparent in the title, which
evokes the elusive mermaids in Eliot's *The Love Song of J. Alfred Prufrock*. Hilary at least *has* literally heard the mermaids and, unlike Prufrock, engaged in life.) Within this novel we glimpse her creative
process. That process surely is unique for each artist, and here we see
that what is essential for Hilary (Sarton, if you will) is to be able to
produce poetry. *Mrs. Stevens* explains Sarton's view of the poetic
process.

First, the muse must be present and must be a woman. Hilary explains to Mar: "I'll tell you the truth. I loved my husband, but . . .
others touched the poet as he did not. It's mysterious" (Sarton's ellipsis;
27). Sarton, of course, has said precisely the same thing over the past
fifteen years as she has answered and reanswered the questions of inter-

viewers. The idea, however, is by no means limited to Sarton and her fictional counterpart, Hilary Stevens. Louise Bogan voices the same idea. On 18 November 1968 Bogan read in the Coolidge Auditorium at the Library of Congress and prefaced "Psychiatrist's Song" (a poem she wrote in 1967) with remarks about age and the visitations of the muse. "The older one gets," she remarked, "the more grateful one is for visits of what used to be called the muse, which certainly exists [audience laughter]. I feel very strongly that it exists. Robert Graves says that women poets have a terrible time—women artists in general—because they have to have a feminine muse [audience laughter]. It hasn't been quite successful to have a masculine one. However, we know what Jung thinks about all that [audience laughter]."[27]

Neither the audience's laughter nor Bogan's offhand reference to Jung lessens her conviction that poets are visited by the muse and that the muse is feminine. Sarton's theory of poetry emerges from the pages of *Mrs. Stevens*. For her and for Hilary Stevens, encounters with women are essential for the inspiration that produces poetry.

The encounter between the teenage Hilary Stevens and her summer tutor, Phillippa Munn, awakens Hilary's sexuality and her poetic gift. As it becomes clear that Phillippa cannot respond sexually to Hilary, the emphasis shifts to poetry. Phillippa unknowingly becomes the muse. Now in her own room (rather than one shared with Phillippa), Hilary spends the night hours pouring verse onto the page of her notebook. The seventy-year-old Hilary remembers that time, and the memory of the sexual scene is direct and effective. Now Hilary marvels that, so young and writing such bad poetry, she nevertheless had recognized the muse:

"Why should I fall in love with you of all impossible people?" As Hilary stood, looking out at the appeasing blue sea, and took a puff of her cigar, that was the phrase that came back to haunt. The sign of the Muse, she thought: impossible, haunting, she who makes the whole world reverberate. Odd that I recognized her at fifteen! And she felt some remote tenderness for that quaking, passionate being whose only outlet had been poetry—bad poetry—bad poetry, at that!—But who had learned then to poise the tensions, to solve the equations through art. (108)

The images come with mathematical precision: tensions must be poised; equations must be solved—not through the right formulae, but through art. (Sarton has always claimed that she has never been able to write in form unless she is inspired, and when the muse has been a felt presence, the poems come.)

The second encounter for Hilary comes much later and is powerful. Hilary falls in love with Willa MacPherson, a woman with two grown sons whose salon evenings attract many visitors—men and women. Hilary's love for Willa brings forth sonnets: "Intensity," she insists, "commands form" (153). And so the sonnet form comes to her with "its implacable demand to clarify, to condense, to bring to fulfillment" (141). As Willa listens to the explanation, she continues to play her role well and, like the true muse, she accepts the poem "with detached, imaginative grace" (141). For Hilary, the process of writing and even of presenting the poems must take place under the influence of the muse—under the fit of inspiration. By the time the poems are to be published, circumstances have radically changed. Indeed, by the time this book of love poems that Willa inspired appears, "as far as Hilary was concerned, it might have been written by someone else" (146).

The sexual part of this encounter occurs on one night when Willa "opened her arms to the child, to the poet, to the lover, and allowed the wave to break. . . . Never again would Hilary experience passion as pure light" (143). The passion had brought forth poems on the one hand, rejection on the other (Willa's door is virtually closed to Hilary). The poet, Sarton says, must eventually pay for the visitations of the muse: "one pays, . . . one is glad to pay" (Sarton's ellipsis; 158).

The third great encounter comes for Hilary in middle age when she falls in love with Dorothea, a sociologist of renown. The love affair is "a secret joy, . . . a source of renewed energy" but carried always the intimate knowledge that "this was a final relationship. There could be no other. But we had turned the Medusa face around and seen our *selves*. The long solitude ahead would be the richer for it" (165, 170). What began as a joyous love affair in middle age deteriorates into a late summer of violent quarrels and accusations. The fury ends the relationship, and with these violent encounters, "the Muse vanished. The poems stopped" (169). The violence and the loss remain in Hilary's mind after all these years. Only in the retrospect possible after years pass can Hilary find any richness from the painful encounter. For Hilary, as she continues to relive her life for the young interviewers, a deeper level of the muse emerges, less explicit than at those times when she was embodied in literal women that Hilary loved. Now the process is less obvious and far more internal as Hilary tries to explain: "Then I began to listen to the silence. Almost without my knowing it, my arid solil-

oquies, those imitation poems, were opening into dialogues. It's *that!*
. . . When the Muse comes back, the dialogue begins. . . . How extraordinary that I never caught onto this obvious fact until now!" (Sarton's ellipsis; 181). The visitations of the muse have been essential, but
costly.

Sarton explores the price exacted to be both artist and woman, to be
a woman with the power that comes with talent. She presents Hilary
Stevens with the familiar dilemma. To be a woman and an artist, Hilary says to the young interviewers, is to become a monster—"we
women who have chosen to be something more and something less
than women!" (156). Hilary argues that women have an inevitable desire for wholeness and balance. Wholeness proves nearly impossible for
the woman artist because she fulfills her role of artist at the expense of
herself. The problem becomes one of power ultimately for the woman.
Whether she is an artist or not she is "haunted by Thurber's cartoon of
the huge threatening and devouring emanation over the house . . .
and, alas, it comes too close to the American man's fear of women"
(Sarton's ellipsis; 173).

In Hilary Stevens Sarton portrays a woman who has survived living
outside the mainstream. Her early novel, a succès de scandale, drove
her mother to declare, "You are not like us, . . . I feel I do not know
you any more" (68). During Hilary's brief marriage to Adrian Stevens
her mother-in-law, Margaret, quickly sees that Adrian and marriage
are not enough for Hilary—the writing will be essential. Margaret
Stevens also discerns the striking difference between herself and Hilary,
sees what she herself has given up and, to her mind at least, gained.
"I settled for being a woman. I wonder whether you can, . . . I have
been blessed with a husband who, if I was unhappy, never knew it,
and if he had known it would not have understood why. . . . There
are enormous comforts in the kind of life I lead" (47–48). Margaret
Stevens's life is not developed in the novel, but Sarton suggests that
she speaks for many women who have ironically found comfort in not
being understood, comfort in concealing their emotions from their
husbands, comfort apparently in an intensely intimate solitude, comfort (particularly for Margaret Stevens) in the garden alone.

After her brief marriage ends with Adrian's fatal accident, Hilary
Stevens has no "normal" woman's role, only those roles that are suspect—that of woman writer ("a contradiction in terms" [111]). The
young woman interviewer wants to know if it is utterly impossible for
a woman writer to lead "a normal life as a woman." It takes Hilary

Stevens several pages finally to give an answer. Women, she says, are by nature expected to bear children, not create works of art. When a woman operates outside this expectation she is, Mrs. Stevens insists, aberrant. If the talent is real, if the woman is a born artist, then she must strive to answer and to fulfill it "at the *expense* of herself as a woman" (191).

The argument has been, as Hilary admits, an exercise in going around the mulberry bush. It is fatal to deny the artist's drive within; it is risky to nurture it. The ultimate capitulation that Hilary makes denies the very essence of the artist and of the woman determined to be and to develop herself. Sarton has the authorial voice add that Hilary "was serious" as she answers Mar's joking words, "You would have liked to be a husband and father, so I've got to be?" To this Hilary says, "No, I think I would have liked to be a woman, simple and fruitful, a woman with many children, a great husband, . . . and no talent!" (Sarton's ellipsis; 219). On the one hand, Hilary sounds like Margaret Stevens who found her comfort in being nothing but what she was supposed to be—a wife who never let her husband suspect that she was unhappy. On the other hand, Hilary's words are simply another way of saying that marriage and children are the enemy of the creative woman. If she wished for husband and children, she wished at the same time to have no talent. A woman cannot, Sarton implies, have it all.

*Mrs. Stevens Hears the Mermaids Singing* is a novel of conversation in the present, of recollected memories, of drawing connections between past and present. Through it all, Mrs. Stevens tells her life and in doing so confronts homosexually boldly—so boldly that when the book was published, Sarton lost her teaching post. (Her agents in London and in New York advised her not to publish this novel; her editor, Eric Swenson, fortunately, encouraged her to do so. See the Appendix.) Sarton's stand is candid, without protest; honest without complaint. What Sarton saw in the relations was passion, love, and joy. But in the sixties (even before the crisis of AIDS cast its awesome presence) the subject matter was risky. Hilary's love for Phillippa, Willa, and Dorothea provides sexual and poetic responses. The affair of Mar and Rufus and Mar's brief encounter with the nameless sailor give Sarton the opportunity to speak out on the subject. Eleven years earlier, in 1954, she had written Louise Bogan a candid explanation of her private and public self: "The *New Yorker* stuff I am doing is easy because I am making no attempt to come to grips with *any* conflict (it would not be for them if I did, and it is not for me at this time. I have to wait for that until I am much older than you because it is all so rather *queer*, you know. I do not wish to be known as a queer person until I am firmly established for central reasons, not a periphery person). I do not think this is a lack of courage, but what I have to say *is* central and I saw how it wrecked . . . [I have omitted the name here] to have people know too much about her private life" (Manuscript letter, 30 January 1954).

Mar has left college, and Rufus (an instructor there) will not now communicate with him. The college reaction had been typical. "Even the fringes of this subject [homosexuality] aroused so much fear, of course, that it was usually mishandled by people in authority, as if they were not dealing with loyalty and love!" (28) For Mar, the encounter had brought great joy and, he emphasizes, no guilt. But Mar's drunken encounter with the sailor takes place in "a crummy hotel" and ends with the sailor stealing his wallet. Now Mar does feel guilty as he tells the episode to Hilary. Her response links the varied advice she has tried to give this troubled young man who is trying to find himself and the poet in him. Hilary argues that affairs of loyalty and love—Mar's encounter with Rufus—are material for poetry; shoddy hotel-room meetings are not. Her conviction is "that you will find what is not material for poetry is not material for life . . . too shallow, don't you know" (Sarton's ellipsis; 212). It is a matter, she says explicitly, of not separating sex and feeling.

As we have seen in others of Sarton's novels, an eccentric old woman is a rich character type, and in *Mrs. Stevens* the seventy-year-old Hilary Stevens dominates. As readers, we may well be inclined to grant Mrs. Stevens the wisdom that comes with age and experience. The present for her is not altogether serene. As artist, she has only recently come to prominence, a state that now brings a flood of letters from readers who often write not to praise her work but to beg her comments on their own and to hear the events of their lives. The recognition so long denied brings problems when it arrives. "So this was fame at last!" Hilary says. "Nothing but a vast debt to be paid to the world in energy, in blood, in time" (58). Old age has also brought the diminishing of physical strength and the diminishing of her own generation. "Everyone, it seemed, was dying. And what really was the point of living on if one was to be the sole survivor of one's world?" (57). As she relives so much of her life through the prompting questions of her interviewers, she conveys the convictions that continue to sustain, convictions that people who live alone and grow old know. "Loneliness is the poverty of self; solitude is the richness of self" (182–83). The distinction makes Hilary Stevens singular. She knows that really to live, one endures suffering and conflict, and when one comes to old age, one must welcome solitude. The living of life and the writing of poetry are central issues, and Sarton treats this subject matter seriously. Even if the resulting novel is flawed, the view of life and of poetry emerges boldly.


## Fables for Readers

Four short works—*The Fur Person, Joanna and Ulysses, The Poet and the Donkey,* and *Miss Pickthorne and Mr. Hare*—fall into that category called the fable or the tale. They are works outside the mainstream of serious fiction, but works that appeal to a wide range of readers. The temptation, of course, is to relegate fiction that centers on animals to the world of children's literature or at least to judge such work as moral tales that do not reverberate on many levels. Indeed, children would delight in Mr. Hare, whose animal name reflects his innocent, skittish, and shy manner. Like real hares, he survives by taking from a "garden"—for Mr. Hare the city dump where he "steals" what other people have "planted" there. These four fables, however, have more serious substance than their titles, dust jackets, and charming illustrations suggest.

A tale, the dictionary tells us, is a synonym for a fable, and a fable, of course, is "a short tale to teach a moral, often with animals as characters." The least successful of Sarton's fables, *The Poet and the Donkey,* is substantially autobiographical. (Sarton did "borrow" a donkey.) The locale is the same village of the retired Latin teacher, Miss Pickthorne, and her curious vagrant neighbor, Trumbull Hare. The poet, Andy Lightfoot, sets out to borrow a donkey and finds an arthritic one named Whiffenpoof, "a magic animal who helps a poet find his poems."[28] However unlikely this episode may be, the book does give one of Sarton's explicit statements about the poet and the muse. In this source lighter by far than *Mrs. Stevens,* Sarton takes up the role of the poet, restating her stand and giving us another glimpse of Sarton the poet.

In his youth Lightfoot found the muse in a tree or in a wave just breaking. As he matured, the muse for him inhabited a person, but not always the same person and not always a person he knew intimately. When the sense of the muse is with him, "it was all he could do to keep up with the poems" (14). If he tries to pin the muse down, tries to bring the magic of inspiration's source into day-to-day living, the muse deserts him. More often than not, the muse inhabits the most

unlikely people and comes to the poet without warning. Totally unaware, she comes to the poet "as an entirely fresh and overwhelming
sensation" (24). The reaction is a description of Andy Lightfoot's (and
Sarton's) poetic life. "The true sign of her spell would always be the
arrival out of the blue of complete lines of poems, and the horror of
her absence was that, without her, he was forced to write entirely in
free verse" (29).

Hetty, Lightfoot's sister, has little patience with such information
and even less with her brother's malaise when the muse no longer "visits" him. Hetty blandly advises Andy "to get over this Muse, as you
call her, and try to find another." Bitterly the poet replies, "One
doesn't *find* a Muse. . . . They come . . . and they don't come often
to dotty old poets, I can tell you" (Sarton's ellipsis; 53). The sister's
disbelief in the power of the muse leads to the point of the book.
Lightfoot will undertake the absurd experiment of restoring the donkey
since it is at least a madness "the world could accept," and the world,
epitomized in sister Hetty, would neither understand nor condone his
desperate appeal for his lost muse—a public figure who is unresponsive
to his attention and to his poetry.

Sarton uses the brief tale to repeat her own dependence on the muse,
to explore the mystery of inspiration, and to indicate the practical results of the mystery. Only with the muse's inspiration can she herself
write in form. *The Poet and the Donkey* suffers from a slight plot and
from characters with "fussy" names. (Is "Lightfoot" a prosodic pun?)
The prosaic sister Hetty is given almost too prosaic a name. And only
a fable can get by with naming the "muse unaware" a "Miss
Hornbeam."

*Joanna and Ulysses,* subtitled "A Tale," has far too much of the fairy
tale. Joanna succeeds too quickly in restoring the abused donkey to
health, finds a small boy's simple question the entrance to her life's
painful past, makes a breakthrough that leads her from being a mere
painter to being a promising artist, effects the altogether unlikely act
of bringing a donkey from its island home to her city apartment building. Too easily people appear to give the donkey an ideal home and
almost too quickly her father—withdrawn for years in passive despair—regains his balance and perspective. Be that as it may, this short
tale succeeds in portraying the lingering suffering caused by World
War II and a strong, independent, single woman unabashed by being
the outsider.

Sarton writes of a thirty-year-old Greek woman who lost her youth with the war. Her indomitable mother had built a network to aid prisoners, and her leadership, well known to the Germans, was considerable. The Germans succeeded in torturing her son and then killed her when she was no use to them or to anyone else. The son lost his hearing from the attack and later cut himself off from all connection with home. The husband, failing at suicide, has for fifteen years wrapped himself in passive despair until Joanna, playing nurse and mother, finally coaxes him from a catatonic state into a simple routine of work and home life. The price has been her youth, independence, happiness, and artistic potential. Now her solitary island vacation provides her awakening as person and as artist. Forced by circumstances to accept domestic and family burdens, she still knows that "somewhere deep down inside her there was a being who was not the dutiful daughter she had forced herself to become."[29] In discovering this essential being, Joanna finally taps the real artist in her as well as embodying that aberrant person, the unmarried woman who happily enjoys an island vacation alone. She baffles the native men who see her there with no companion—but not herself.

The restoration of the ill-used donkey (expensive ointment, bandages, food) could easily have made the tale a sentimental episode. But Sarton prevents this by having Joanna laugh at the absurdity of her experiment and by presenting her act as a gesture against the "endless chain of violence" that ravages the world. (In *At Seventy*, written during 1982–83, Sarton repeats this theme: "The hardest thing we are asked to do in this world is to remain aware of suffering, suffering about which we can do nothing" [232].) Joanna has been powerless to prevent the disaster to her own family. In rescuing the donkey from owners who would literally have worked the beast to his death, Joanna interrupts that endless chain. Her gesture is one made in a world where, Sarton writes, "one has had to witness too much suffering about which nothing could be done" (82). Sarton does not take Joanna's gesture lightly. Her own youth had been disrupted when her parents were forced to leave their lovely Belgian home at the outset of World War I, and during World War II she knew the details of suffering and deprivation that her friends in Europe endured.

The most charming and appealing of these fables is *The Fur Person*. Early in the fifties May Sarton and Judith Matlack sublet their Cambridge house at 9 Maynard Place to Vladimir and Vera Nabokov. They also "sublet" the household cat, Tom Jones, "the fur person." Thus this cat is immortalized by his real and surrogate owners, who are most certainly numbered among "'the fervent lovers and austere scholars' whom Baudelaire called the particular friends of cats."[30]

Sarton's preface declares that this book was intended for grandmothers to read aloud to whole families. Indeed, the techniques of rhymed verses, alliterative passages, and catalogs call for the spoken voice. The reading aloud would also draw attention to the frequently amusing burlesque passages which abound. For instance, Tom Jones "was in the kitchen, spirited there as Odysseus into the arms of Circe by the ineffable cod" (21). And the particular friends of cats read with satisfaction the accurate descriptions of a cat and his habits. When a cat does decide to sleep, the first line of his "song" inextricably mixes into "a purr and his suddenly making himself into a round circle of peace, all kneading spent, and one paw over his nose" (49).

The adventures of the Fur Person (and a trip to the vet) lead him to a metamorphosis—from Tom Jones, the cat obliged to fight, to "the Fur Person," the cat happy to stay in the sun. The change effected brings forward the point of the fable: "The Fur Person learned then and there that it is better to be a philosopher than to be a king and that, all things considered, wisdom was to be preferred to power" (101). *The Fur Person* entertains, charms, and teaches. Its appeal—at least to Baudelaire's "fervent lovers and austere scholars"—is lasting.

Readers of Sarton's journals know her own abiding affection for cats—especially the remarkable cat whose name was Bramble. Sarton's father shared her delight in cats, naming various ones of his own Gus, Cloudy, and the Harvard Cat. His regular letters to May Sarton often contain reports of the present cat's exploits—reports juxtaposed to news of his lecture engagements, journal editing, travel plans. From a summer retreat he wrote to Sarton in 1939 that "The Harvard Cat is most intelligent; she has learned to travel in the lift, and will not walk a single flight up if she can help it. She meows for the lift, and when she has reached the floor where her business calls her, meows again!" (Manuscript letter, 16 July 1939). The whimsy of this anecdote suffices. It is the detail of ordinary living that remains important, for it is that sense of detail and reality of living that continues to make Sarton's fiction so appealing. It certainly is the detail that has made her memoirs and journals appeal to thousands as they have watched a real person expose the raw nerves of living and writing, watched her share the triumphs of love, nature, life.

## Always the Strong Woman

Because of her European birthplace and her parents' forced exile to
America, Sarton has always felt a sense of dislocation. Even though she
has lived most of her life in America, she continues to have that sense
of lacking a permanent locale and milieu. Perhaps this sense of disso-
ciation from where she lived most of her life accounts for the occasional
social satire, especially of Boston manners. At times the touch is light
as in *Shadow of a Man,* which occasionally echoes Eliot's tone in "The
Boston Evening Transcript." This success in light satire manifests her
gift of humor, a trait rarely mentioned in reviews or in critical discus-
sions of her work.

Early in *Shadow of a Man* Persis's funeral occurs and introduces the
expectation of ritual and Bostonian responses. Collectively to Boston-
ians, "death was one of their favorite exercises; all the concealed love
of drama could now have free play."[31] Persis is buried in King's Chapel
where sit "innumerable faded intelligent women, under those hats pe-
culiar to Boston, designed to conceal rather than reveal the personality
of the wearer" (59). The tone suggests that Sarton shares the widower
Alan's view, "for Alan did not hate Boston, he appreciated it—but
laughed just the same. The Chinese have their ceremonies he thought
and Boston has its Famous Quotations. And what would we do without
them?" (25).

It is the visiting relatives who provide the most humor. Dorcas sips
her sherry after the funeral and says quite cheerfully, "It takes a death
in the family to bring us to Boston" (67). When the cousins from
Newburyport learn that Francis's (Persis's son) friend Saul comes from
the remote reaches of Detroit, the conversation turns to the memories
and habits that have dominated their lives. None of the clan has ever
gone to Detroit, but "Papa once went as far as Denver, in 1910, wasn't
it Lucy?" Her sister adds, as if it might enlighten the entire room, "He
climbed Pike's Peak" (66). The geographic lapse and the unspoken
dismay that Francis's friend is Jewish simply lead the sisters back to
their main theme, the news of their ninety-five-year-old father whose
care is their lives. Eagerly, they report the latest news. "He has trouble
with his digestion. . . . The death of the *Transcript* was a great blow
to him" (66).

The stuffiness and banal concerns are presented with humor and
contrast sharply with the major themes in the novel. Sarton's attention
here is on Francis Adams Chabrier, twenty-six, who finally comes of

age. As the novel opens, he is arrogant, intellectual, sexually imma-
ture. His affluent surroundings, his romantic father's early death, and
his relationship with strong women (especially his mother Persis) have
for all their respective richness impeded his development. It is only
through a passionate love affair with his mother's contemporary and
close friend, Solange, that Francis finally discovers who he is, accepts
adulthood, chooses a profession. The affair with the older woman (oed-
ipal indeed in this instance) ironically brings Francis to terms with Ann
Winthrop, a sensible and bright young woman whom he doubtless will
marry.

But the novel is also about women—women's independence, strong
women's lives. Persis Adams Chabrier Bradford dies as the novel begins, but this extraordinary woman dominates the book. Her early
married years were lived in Paris, giving her "a confidence in herself
which Boston women of her background often lack" (8). Her independence means that above all she will have her freedom. She even keeps
her musical talent for her pleasure because "a concert artist is always a
slave" (7). She was not the stereotypic wife to either of her husbands.
Her embattled, detached, but indispensable relation with her son
meant that she was not a nurturing maternal figure. She was, for him,
the epitome of order and intellect—the ideal woman he finds at last in
Solange.

The central image in the novel (a large plaster statue of a woman
nude to the waist sitting with legs crossed and a baby in her arms)
represents the conflicting sexual/maternal needs at war in Francis. The
resolution comes in the affair with Solange, the surrogate mother who
becomes his lover. In an obvious, but not especially successful way, the
statue also represents the sophistication of Europe. That milieu would
be struck with the beauty and power of the statue, while in America a
large white object, the novel suggests, would call forth veneration because it was a Frigidaire.

Finally, this novel shows one of Sarton's strongest points: the ability
to devise and represent a great variety of highly individual and interesting characters—particularly women. The main characters are complemented by excellent minor ones. There is Fonatanes, the talented
man of the theater; Persis's sister Alison who lives on a tenth of her
income and supports sensible causes with the rest; and Alan Bradford's
impossible mother, a true Thurber woman who could be terrifying in
her gentleness. And, of course, Solange, who enters the affair with
Francis knowing that "she must be wise since he could not be" (162)

and who learns now for herself what solitude after her husband's death had meant, "I never shall quite live again. That's what I didn't know" (224). It is a hard frontier that many women in Sarton's novels must meet. Solange looks at her face, confronting the difficulty of growing old, of all the years to come, of the loneliness. The great loss of love has no compensating force in Solange's life. She, more than almost any other of Sarton's women characters, confronts the coming on of age with the full dread of loneliness. She is indeed an independent and strong woman, but she is also vulnerable to the pain and risk that independence and inevitable loss bring. Sensuous and so appealing, Solange represents the women characters who cross Sarton's pages, echoing many of their sentiments, living their expectations, suggesting always that life be lived fully, knowing always that in the end what we have is solitude.

In June of 1931 the young May Sarton was in Europe. As would be her habit for many years, she visited the Limbosch family whose friendship extended back to her childhood. From their Belgian farm she wrote to her parents on 25 June, sending a letter that links her earliest memories (the house in Belgium) with the present (the Limbosch farm which was a second home) and with the future (her lifetime as a writer living in houses she herself would establish): "I'm sitting at my table (which came from Wondelgem) looking out over orange and purple and green trees toward the field and an orange gable. *I shall write volumes* (Manuscript letter, 25 June [1931]; my italics).

## Chapter Four

# "Expensive Commodities": The Poems

Poems are, May Sarton wrote to Louise Bogan in 1955, "expensive commodities, as you well know" (Manuscript letter, 12 October 1955).[1] In 1937 Sarton published her first book of poems, *Encounter in April;* her most recent, a chapbook entitled *The Phoenix Again* in 1987; and *The Silence Now* in 1988. This half century for Sarton has brought forth some sixteen volumes of poetry, a body of work characterized by effective themes, diverse subject matter, and varied poetic forms. Consistently, she has declared that poetry is more important to her than the novels, memoirs, or journals. To poetry she would give her attention and in poetry she would prefer her reputation to be. Such has not been the case. The steady reading public for her journals dominates, and although Sarton has for many years been included in poetry anthologies, her poetry has not commanded attention in academic circles. The oeuvre, however, is impressive and the earliest volumes hold up especially well.

Sarton has always written poetry, even during her late teens and early twenties when she sought to make a career in the theater. She has always claimed the necessity of a muse without whose presence the poems did not come. And she has frequently acknowledged that her forte—the lyric poem—has long been out of fashion. Of late (especially in her public interviews), Sarton has said that her many love affairs are in the poetry. Seriously claiming the muse, writing much lyric poetry, and acknowledging lesbian relationships are reasons that some critics have been less than enthusiastic about her poems. From the beginning, however, Sarton was published and enjoyed favorable critical reviews. But from the sources where she would most like to be praised—the *New Yorker* during Louise Bogan's thirty-eight-year tenure as poetry critic, the powerful *New York Times,* and the established academic community—praise generally has not been abundant.

In the mid-forties Sarton was in Santa Fe, a place she found conducive to writing. She was at this time taking stock, looking carefully and critically at the poems. In a letter to William Theo Brown she explains her current dissatisfaction with her poems. The fault she saw clearly lay in what she called "a sort of romantic over-emphasis" that led her to write "such personal poems." Although she was attempting to write in form and to control the poems, the fact remained that this "is the way they come and I do not seem to think abstractly very much. I can imagine a wonderful poem about a rock or a tree but when I come to write, the old romantic fallacy pops up, and there I am talking about myself and my own sensations as usual!" (Manuscript letter, 24 June 1945). The "romantic fallacy" is never fully conquered, and much of her poetry continues to remain personal. But her own clear assessment of her poems is important: from early in her career she has been quite aware of her strengths as well as her weaknesses.

The appearance of *Selected Poems of May Sarton* in 1978 provided the opportunity for a retrospective. The editors chose to emphasize theme rather than chronology and made their purpose "to preserve and to clarify the central rhythms of the poet's voice and vision."[2] A chronological reading of Sarton's poetry, however, is most instructive, and one discovers that her poetic gift is strong at the very beginning, reaches its fullest strength in *A Private Mythology* (1966), *A Grain of Mustard Seed* (1971), and *A Durable Fire* (1972), and continues well into the more recent volumes *Halfway to Silence* (1980) and *Letters from Maine* (1984). The sweep of the poetry reveals that her strong concerns and themes were present at the beginning: an affinity with nature (especially the flower garden), the ectasy of love and the despair of lost love, the permanent cycle of growth and change, the deep response to music and to art, the necessity of silence (this later becomes the passion for solitude), and what I call the presence of "women's poems."

As her experiences change and broaden, especially through travel, Sarton's poetry takes up additional subject matter and themes when these experiences have been distilled. *A Private Mythology (1966)* (dedicated to "my students at Wellesley College, 1960–1964") drew on a journey Sarton made to Japan and India. The poems respond to the exotic and to the ceremonies observed in strange places, and she writes of "A Private Mythology–I," which later in the volume is complemented with "A Private Mythology–II," poems about her return to the New England landscape and the seasonal experiences of drought, snowstorms, and the extended cold in New Hampshire. She completes these two "private mythologies" by forcing memory to a redistillation in the last poem, "Second Thoughts on the Abstract Gardens of Japan." Now, those "artful images" of Japan "trouble my thought" and she finds disturbing images: "Clearly, we can but sense some peril / In a stone waterfall? / Made of hard rocks, and absolutely sterile." And now this waterfall is fossilized, a "static death." The experience remembered is a negative one since "motion deprived of motion always will / Suggest despair." For all its beauty and order, the memory now finds the famous Japanese garden "too formalized." The preference is for the "quaint New England wilderness" and the coalescing of wildness and creativity. "My garden, so untamed, still has not lacked / Its hard-won flowers." Returned home, the poet claims her own posture—"Unbuttoned ego. I have staked / My life on controlled native powers"—and further claims that she needs "good violence to find organic form."[3]

A special importance lies in part 1 of *A Grain of Mustard Seed: New Poems (1971),* which presents nine poems that are Sarton's public response to the social and political trauma of the sixties. Alicia Ostriker discusses the significance of much important political poetry that emerged from the women's movement and the era was not, she argues, "simply political. Apolitical poets such as May Swenson, Elizabeth Bishop, and May Sarton, for example, are of the highest relevance when we ask questions about the relation of women and nature, women and creativity, women and myth."[4] Certainly Sarton has not written the moving political poems that her close friend, Muriel Rukeyser, did. Nor has she undertaken the long sweeping free-verse lines of Rukeyser. However, these particular nine poems, as well as Sarton's private actions, suggest that at heart May Sarton *is* a very political person.

The opening poem, "Ballad of the Sixties," pictures violent disharmony in all parts of the country, a time of chaos. "For only the mad are sane, / And only the lost are well, / And loss of fire the bane / Of this season in Hell." Other poems center on violence to children, the wave of political assassinations and the shootings at Kent State, the prejudice against blacks, and the paradigm of all twentieth-century suffering, the Holocaust. (When Sarton writes of the shooting at Kent State, she entitles the poem "We'll to the Woods No More, The Laurels Are Cut Down," using a nursery rhyme every French schoolchild would have known. She juxtaposes the nursery-rhyme meter with the shocking words that "children" are being killed.) Her outrage and horror are epitomized and paradoxically balanced with hope in her long poem,

"The Invocation to Kali." Only when violence and shame are fully realized can any change be effected; only by invoking Kali, the Black Goddess, can darkness be dispelled. Sarton, indeed, describes herself as a political person aware of and responsive to the world's dilemmas. We see in these poems the same response she exhibited during World War II when she joined in volunteer work at home and provided as much relief as possible for friends in Europe who were sharply deprived during the war years. One year after *A Grain of Mustard Seed* Sarton published *A Durable Fire,* and here the subject matter leaves social protest per se, as we shall see, and returns to the subjects of nature, love, grief, and despair.

In these three volumes Sarton can be seen as a versatile poet (in subject matter and in form) and as a person whose public image and private self are both fully engaged in the art and process of writing poetry. Active political and social issues return as subject matter in scattered poems, but not again in a large cluster like the sixties poems.[5] This fact suggests that the poetic impulse simply has led Sarton in other directions and does not reflect diminished concern for local and general suffering. Eudora Welty (born in the same decade as Sarton) has responded well to the writer's burden in times of turmoil when the public demands that artists respond. The writer's response to the immediate, Welty says, is virtually impossible unless the response takes the form of satire and assumes the mode of the poem or the drama. Without the scaffolding of satire, the zeal for reform "has never done fiction much good." In the sixties Welty claimed for herself a spirit of goodwill; that is, a disposition that protested violence and injustice. "But good will all by itself," she adds, "can no more get a good novel written than it can paint in watercolor or sing Mozart."[6] Sarton's nine poems of social protest are not satiric, and they did not at the time provide rallying points for protesters. They do, however, succeed in conveying one poet's deep response to the times, a protest expressed in the words and events of that era. In "The Ballad of Ruby" *(A Grain of Mustard Seed),* based on a child's story in Robert Coles's 1967 volume *Children in Crisis,* Sarton portrays the peril for black children facing life in integrated schools for the first time. The poem has us watch Ruby: "Her mother dressed the child in white, / White ribbons plaited in her hair, / And sent her off to school to fight." Sarton's words speak genuine concern as did her participation in various programs and readings for black audiences in Boston. Her deep sense of justice and injustice goes deep.

## The Role of the Poet

Above all, Sarton makes her role as poet primary, always interrupting any other writing if "a poem comes." In the forties her correspondence with Basil de Selincourt[7] reveals useful remarks about the poet's role, at a time when Sarton valued de Selincourt's opinions and judgment. Perhaps not the ideal reader of Sarton (a major poem like "My Sisters, O My Sisters" in *The Lion and the Rose* did not apparently interest him), de Selincourt nevertheless wrote passages in letters that define the essence of Sarton as poet. In a letter dated 15 April [1945?] he writes about form, Sarton's emotional center, and her emerging independence—his letter remains a useful commentary on Sarton's poetic life:

"But after all, May, the value of forms is nothing except to carry the meaning further and *longer,* and help us to sort out meanings that come and go from those that stay with us. What I most treasure in your work is that you seem more and more to be establishing your emotional center on the enduring human values—and the feeling of a dedication grows in what you write. With this must come too a sacred impulse to write in such a way that your vision is truly communicated—allowing no trick of whim or fancy to intrude. I still find your poems a little difficult. I believe that when you are surer still of what you mean, you will be a little less Valérian or Rilkish, or whatever also suggests the abstruse."

Sarton has not found her poetic "emotional center" in political or social issues although she has cared sincerely about many issues. Instead she has found her enduring voice and has made her contribution by centering her role as poet in poems about and for women, by using the garden and flowers as metaphor for unfailing variety and inevitable growth, by writing well of old age and of the death of those one loves, and, most of all, in being a poet who does not exhaust the images and metaphors and emotions of love poems.

In her essay "The School of Babylon" Sarton sees "the poetic player" (as she says Valéry expressed it in a different context) as consciously choosing his game, or his conscious role as poet. Some, she says, "prefer roulette, others chess. If you are a chess player, what you are looking for is a new opening, a new device by which you may win within the old rules; a means of taking your opponent by surprise. The dynamics of form have to do with our intimate relation with the past, and our natural instinct for what we can use for a particular poem, the form

that can best become a vehicle for its electric current, the tension between the whole rich past and the poem now" (*WW,* 9). The image of
games is instructive, and Sarton's most successful poems show her consciously choosing and working to maintain an approach and a comple-
mentary form—choosing, as it were, the game and her role as proper
player. An undated and untitled page in the Sarton Papers contains
notes jotted down for one of the many poetry courses she taught. No
commentary accompanies the list to suggest the order of importance,
but the list as a whole embodies the underlying principles she holds as
poet:

*Poetry Courses*

freshness of imagery

sound of sense

point of view

suspense

rhythm

repeated pattern

————[?] of the unexpected

The fullest expression of Sarton's poetics and her literal process of
writing poems is found in the 1980 gathering of lectures/essays, published as *Writings on Writing.* The views and the techniques emerge
there from roots present very early. In 1938, just one year after her
first book of poems was published, Sarton reflects on what rules govern
the writing of poems. In a letter to her friend, S. S. Koteliansky, she
attempts to explain and concludes with a telling image to indicate that
formulating rules is virtually impossible:

Making rules for poetry is rather like finding an anatomy for a chimera[,] for
every simple statement leads one finally to the most mysterious and strange
places, and if one does manage for a second to hold the chimera in hand and
feels its cones[,] it changes shape so fast that the fox is a unicorn before you
can say "There!" (Manuscript letter, 9 October 1938)

A surer attempt at analyzing her poetic technique comes some ten
years later in a letter to the artist, William Theo Brown. The image
now is not the skeleton of an elusive mythological beast but instead a
method borrowed from art and applied to poetry: "I was interested to

see somewhere that Matisse begins with a literal rendering of an object
or person and then gradually reduces it to its essence, drawing by drawing. That is the way I write poems, but many people carry the changes
in their heads and many painters I'm sure make the abstractions in
their heads too. It is all fascinating" (Manuscript letter, 26 January
1947). The attention to the literal rendering that then undergoes
changes and versions to reach its "essence" suggests a poet at work for
whom method and revision are altogether as essential as the inspiration
claimed from the muse. When Sarton articulates in a lecture/essay the
process and the technique required to produce a poem, she is precise
and analytic. "The School of Babylon," "The Writing of a Poem," and
"Revision as Creation" embody her theory of poetics and, as brief critical treatises, they deserve attention. Her primary theme—the creating
and balancing of tension in the poem—is expressed quite well through,
as we have seen, the metaphor of games. I quote at length because
these passages provide a base for much of Sarton's work, a base that has
remained consistent:

> But I hope it goes without saying that, just as the joy of playing tennis for
> the player is the mastery of the continual stress of the game, and if it were
> easier to play, it would not be half as much fun, so the poet of course is never
> happier, nor more wholly himself, than when he is engaged in the play of
> writing a poem, in making the puzzle come out 'right.' And the longer he
> can tease it along, the happier he is, if he is a poet like Valéry. Of course there
> is the final danger of crossing the intangible frontier beyond which a poem is
> damaged by mere manipulation . . . it may suddenly go dead like the mouse
> which the cat has played with. When is a poem finished? The answer is, I
> think, when all the tensions it has posited are perfectly equilibrated, when
> the change of a single syllable would so affect the structure that the poem
> would fall like a house of cards under the shift. (*WW*, 19, ellipsis Sarton's)

Sarton has referred to her poems as going through hundreds of drafts,
and she claims (with Valéry, as she points out) that revision is the most
interesting phase because that provides such a journey of discovery (see
"Revision as Creation," *WW*, 59–66).

If the tension is to be realized, then the image, the metaphor, must
be inevitable and "complex enough to carry the weight of complete
feeling; it must be absolutely exact" ("Revision as Creation," *WW*, 60).
Sarton considers that an image she jotted down from the writings of
the French psychologist, Gaston Bachelard, exemplifies such a metaphor. The image—"Salt dissolves and crystallizes; it is a Janus mate-

rial"—became the starting point for her poem, "In Time Like Air."
The early stanza examines salt's properties; it dissolves in water and it
crystallizes in air. The image then leads to the point Sarton makes
about the nature of love and time. What element, stanza 3 asks, "dissolves the soul / So it may be both found and lost?" The answer comes
in the next stanza where the image of the Janus-like salt now becomes
the growing and changing capacities of love:

> Love, in its early transformation,
> And only love, may so design it
> That the self flows in pure sensation,
> Is all dissolved, and found at last
> Without a future or a past,
> And a whole life suspended in it.[8]

The tension must also be reflected in the form of the poem. Although Sarton has written free verse, she has by far preferred writing
in strict form. Four volumes have sonnet sequences; one of these, the
twenty sonnets that comprise "A Divorce of Lovers" in *Cloud, Vine,
Leaf, Stone* (1961), represents a considerable achievement. In addition,
Sarton has frequently written in terza rima, in the ballad stanza, in
rhymed couplets, and in many other rhymed patterns. For example,
"A Last Word" is comprised of eight five-line stanzas, rhyming *a b c d
b;* "An Intruder" is eight tercets, rhyming *a a a;* "Evening Walk in
France" is eleven couplets; "Dutch Interior" is ten tercets rhyming *a b
a;* "A Parrot" is three eight-line stanzas rhyming *a a b c a b c b.* Sarton
has worked to use traditional poetic forms and worked skillfully. The
list of underlying principles for her teaching assignment includes
"rhythm" and "repeated patterns." She has demonstrated in poem after
poem that strict form is her most natural poetic inclination.

## Poems of America, Poems from Abroad

Sarton's deep feeling of exile—her European parents, her divided
loyalty between Europe and America, her never feeling completely part
of a locale—runs deep. The uprooting of the family from the idyllic
Wondelgem caused a feeling of dislocation that never faded altogether.
Nevertheless, Sarton has lived almost all of her life in America, and
the American poems, especially those in *The Lion and the Rose* (1948),
document her coming of age as an American. Traveling by car, her
eight-month journey across America in 1940–41 was organized around

visits to colleges where, for expenses and a modest honorarium, Sarton lectured and read her poems. The Sarton Papers include materials from this period: her lecture notes for "Journey Toward America," a list of thirty-one poem titles, and portions of unfinished poems. In the list of poems ten appear that will later be collected as the section, "American Landscapes" in *The Lion and the Rose*. These American poems were written as she traveled south from Cambridge into Virginia, the Carolinas, Mississippi, across Texas, and then farther west with an extended stay in Santa Fe. It is as interested traveler that she responds to the history of Winchester, Virginia, and as she takes in the elegance of Monticello. "All the joy of invention and of craft and wit / Are freely granted here, all given rein, / But taut with the classic form and ruled by it, / Elegant, various, magnificent—and plain / Europe become implacably American!"[9]

Guilford College, North Carolina, is celebrated as are the Charleston plantations that Sarton associates with the far past, the remnant of a single century of rice plantations whose flourishing is past. Natchez, Texas, Boulder Dam, the Colorado mountains, are other geographic subjects as Sarton sees and claims America. The New Mexico poems, however, are the most effective, simply because she stayed there long enough to acquire a sense of the landscape and to observe closely the rituals like the Indian corn dances. The concluding poem of the series is "Poet in Residence—Carbondale, Illinois," which begins with a scathing portrayal of place and people:

> But ignorant of man's long ecstasy and pain,
> You come to books as to a strange dull town
> Where you know no one by name and do not care,
> And never recognize the Waste Land as your own.
>
> I looked behind you and saw nothing, nothing at all,
> But a flat empty wall,
> I saw you lonely and bored walking in a dull town;
> I saw you letting the books fall.
>
> And then because there was nothing else to do,
> I saw you turning on the radio.
>
>                                   (31)

As poet, she is a stranger in the "center of America," thoroughly frustrated to find no response to her passion for poetry: "How can the books be broken to yield the dynamic answer, / And we embody

thought in living as does the dance, the dancer?" She senses her failure—why be a poet if she cannot kindle a response to her art? In reflection, Sarton as the poet in residence realizes that what she herself
learned about poetry as a child had been long years metamorphosing.
"All that was abstract become concrete / Is part of you like an eyelash
or your hair." This discovery leads to a far more tolerant view of the
present students and also to Sarton's encompassing view of teaching
poetry. The experience of the moment may require years before it becomes an experience that informs and enriches life:

> Imagine a moment when student and teacher
> (Long after the day and the lesson are over)
> Will soar together to the pure immortal air
> And find Yeats, Hopkins, Eliot waiting there.
> But you understand, it cannot happen yet.
> It takes a long time to live what you learn.
>
> (35)

The poem ends with the poet reconciled to the brutal landscape and
weather, finding there gifts, finding in the students promise. Like
Yeats's wandering Aengus, Sarton has been the "Stranger with a fire in
your head"; however, she ends the poem with objectivity and satisfaction. "So what you gave was given and what you taught was learned,
/ Striking rock for water and the water falling from air, / Opening a
door to find someone in the room, already there" (36).

In concluding the section, "American Landscapes," this poem, "Poet
in Residence," places Sarton in roles that she has maintained all of her
life: traveler, teacher, poet. Further, the section brings together these
experiences as she discovers more of America than the academic world
of Cambridge, Massachusetts, and the city life of New York. If there
is not a full rapport with the entire country, there is an appreciation
for its landscape, its own history,[10] and its people. The opening lines
of "Colorado Mountains" (a poem of four quatrains) represent Sarton's
response to the new landscape she encounters. "Plain grandeur escapes
definition. You / Cannot speak about the mountains well." Here she
does not attempt concrete particularity, but rather conveys the grandeur through the general "clear plane" and "sharp shadow" and "sheer
cliff." In late travel poems her eye will settle upon the particular, but
here the sense of sweep and space (the "Texas poems") and grandeur
suggests new experiences that prompt the poet to write.

Manuscripts from this period include drafts that have never been published. Of particular interest is a long poem that has three preliminary divisions—"Voice of the Mind," "Voice of the Shop Girl," "Voice of Harvard Boy." Extant lines include the section, "Voice of the Shop Girl," which establishes the voice of a working girl whose experience contrasts completely with Sarton, the traveler about America. Although Sarton frequently writes about working people (especially her neighbors in Nelson, New Hampshire), praising them in prose and in poems, she never returns to this particular voice. Here we get a depressing "women's poem," a portrait of the working girl whose expectations are grounded in the moment, who cares not at all for the life of travel and adventure, who cannot imagine being impressed with the Colorado mountains or Monticello. Her America is the cosmetic counter and the local bar. The sound of the voice is real as it speaks one version of the American dream:

> I worked my way through college to get
> This job behind a counter selling face-cream
> To women who never read a book yet.
> I'd advise you, kid, to go tell your dream
> To Joan Crawford. Her feet don't ache.
> But let me tell you right now at the end
> Of my day I don't ask anything to give or take
> But a couple of dry martinis with the boy-friend.
> I've never seen the whole god-given country
> You're so nuts about but leave me out of it,
> You can have the rivers for a dime from me,
> I can do without those mountains and love it.
> And I'm just a little fed up on red, white, and blue
> Compacts and that eternal Ballad for Americans,
> aren't you?[11]

Clearly, Sarton was not. But the provincial, city-centered voice of the shop girl places her with the millions who would not be moved by the plains and the mountains that Sarton celebrates in American landscapes.

Poems emanate from Sarton's frequent sojourns to Europe, especially from the French and Belgian countryside, from sites like Chartres Cathedral, from familiar haunts, too, in England. When she neared her fiftieth birthday, she took an extended trip to the East—to Japan and India—ending this journey with a stay in Greece. She wrote Muriel

Rukeyser on 8 May 1965 that "there will be new poems in early '66. I am at last writing the poems about Japan and Greece. It has taken 3 years from them to rise up" (Manuscript letter, 8 May 1965). Sarton had begun work on these poems the previous December during a stay at Yaddo and had run into difficulty. "The problem is," she wrote to Basil de Selincourt, "that they do not want to come in form and I find free verse exhausting as one seems to be able to go on revising forever— there are no walls and everything slides around" (Manuscript letter, 6 December 1964).

The poems (in "Private Mythology-I") begin with "A Child's Japan" where Sarton summons early childhood memories in Cambridge where her image of holiness was Kobo Daishi. "Young and beautiful, / Sitting on his lotus / In a thin gold circle / Of light. / He is with me still." Characteristics of her family suggest an affinity with the child's idea of Japan: her father bent over his work, abandoning his family in fantasy to follow his pure love of monasteries; her artist mother, capable always of transferring a small room of "clutter and confusion" into something open and quiet. The immediate landscape—rain, snow on black branches—the "sweet austerity" and the "extravagance of work" within this household move Sarton to say how Japanese it looked and to think "It is clear to me now / That we were all three / A little in love with Japan" (17–18).

Now as an adult, having outlived her parents, she travels to that far eastern land, feeling herself a distant relative, "flying home to Japan." The poems that follow document the pleasure of her experiences and center in minute particularities. For example, in "A Country House" Sarton pictures a Japanese house and its garden of twelve plum trees. When the paper wall slides back, one floats between "house and garden." In "Kyoko" Sarton balances the delicacy of the woman's name ("Kyoko" means apricot and she, like that fruit, was "delicate, transparent") with the reality of the war ("Disaster / Shadows her cheek / Like the falling plum blossom"). It is the lightness and delicacy of ritual and ceremony that vitalize the poems: the precise order of drinking tea (one turns the cup around "two-and-a-half times"), the process of gift exchange, the pleasure in the sound of strange words, the gardens. In a brief two-stanza poem entitled "Shugaku-In, Imperial Villa" Sarton uses an odd fact from a guide book as the epigraph. She turns from the humor she then creates in stanza 1 ("not a single poem to wash!") to the seriousness in stanza 2 when the speaker responds fully to "smell and taste":

### Shugaku-In, Imperial Villa

*"Shensi-Dai* means platform to wash a poem.
The veranda may have been used in brushing up
poetic ideas, while hearing the sound of Male Waterfalls near here." Guide Book

1

I seemed to sense a flight of poems
Like a flight of cranes
Disappearing over the waterfalls
(Male and female)
And perhaps settling
In the rough ploughed field next door,
While the ghost of an emperor
In an attitude of willed quiescence,
Mixes the ink
And arranges the brushes in vain—
Not a single poem to wash!

(26)

In "Japanese Prints," a series of twelve poems, Sarton tries her hand
at haiku and achieves some sense of that form so associated with the
Japanese poets. Then in "Wood, Paper, Stone," she discovers, as if for
the first time, the beauty possible in these natural elements, used to
such perfection in Japanese dwellings. By comparison, all contrived
things—including the haiku itself—are less to be admired:

Even the poem,
Hedged in by the appropriate,
Ceased to breathe:
The haiku ends
In mannerism

(35)

Mindful that she is the Westerner, the outsider, Sarton reflects in "Inn
at Kyoto" on herself as traveler. Among the slight Japanese she feels
her size ("like an elephant"), her own middle age, her coming so far
alone, her acknowledging that East and West are different. The experience has been rich, and these travel poems of Japan find their center
in these lines: "I inhabit a marvelous world / Where every sense is

taught / New ways of perceiving." And perhaps it is the *poet* whose senses can quicken to new ways of perceiving and of perceiving new ways of seeing the old.

Themes repeated throughout the poems on India are the "staggering variety" of the pilgrims, the multitudes in motion ("Walking, walking. / It has no beginning. It never ends"), the atmosphere of heavy air that seems to retard even the simplest activity ("Notes from India"). A brief vignette in "Notes from India" illustrates Sarton's ability to observe carefully and to transform the moment into the poem. (Reviewing *A Private Mythology* in the *New York Times Book Review,* Joseph Bennet found the India poems "remarkable for their savage brilliance.") At a place called Fathpur Sikir time has changed the site from the aristocratic sport of falconry to the banal entertainment of dancing monkeys, and one senses the loss of dignity on several levels:

> 4. At Fathpur Sikir
> Where once the Moghul princes
> Rode with falcons on their wrists,
> An old man
> Sings a song
> To make two monkeys dance.
>
> (42)

The section of travel poems ends with her arrival in Greece, a return to the West and to the familiar. During her journey she has been a stranger to family life and turns now with pleasure to a family meal in Greece. Here she is no longer an outsider and contents herself with the pleasure in this setting, these familiar surroundings—white roses, lemon trees, "two expansive figs."

Sarton's travel poems do more than record visits to faraway places. They show the sensitivity of the poet to observe and perceive. When the experience goes deep and then returns in a poem, we witness her full assimilation of what she has seen, heard, felt. Perhaps the key to all of Sarton's many travel poems lies in the opening lines of "Notes from India." Responding to the poet's travel letters, a friend asks (in the poem): "You describe so much / But how do you feel? / What is happening to you?" The poet answers, "What I *see* is happening to me" (my italics). Travel for Sarton has never been a static experience, but the vital seeing of a traveler who participates in all that surrounds her at the moment.

## The Transition of Death

Few themes have engaged Sarton's attention as have old age and death; here some of her best poems speak with clarity and feeling. It is the evident intensity of these poems that commends them and makes regrettable the effusive praise some of her critics have given. Particularly regrettable are the exaggerations. "Her technical, intellectual, and temperamental scope is such as to launch her into the environs of greatness." Or to claim, as this same critic does, that because "In Kashmir" is written in tercets and "the metrical foot of the first stanza is dactylic, the beat of Virgil's *Aeneid,* and the lines are in trimeter, exactly half the length of Virgil's hexameter," this twenty-four-line poem "is to be a epic in miniature."[12] Sarton's good poems stand up well to reading and analysis; her work is ill served by exaggerated claims, and her poems on old age and death are prime examples of poems that stand on their artistic merit.

Sarton writes well about death both in the general sense of loss and in the acute suffering of personal grief. In a poem like "The Puritan" death is not centered on a person but in the broad and irrevocable loss of the landscape. The time is gone when the Puritan was "seduced by the soft luxurious hill"; now there are bare pastures, thin harvests, a bitter land where even a child learns to be fearful and wary. The death imagery in nature continues in "From a Train-Window" where the speaker sees "a world grown old," the landscape "the picture of a world bitten with blight." The sharp alliteration underscores the despair. Loss is, of course, felt even more when people grow old and face death, and Sarton admires the old, claims for them a revered place as age advances them toward death. It is the old "who have learned the sovereign ease," who are "the great transparencies." Youth, on the other hand, "is too vulnerable to bear the tide." And it is through these old people—brave and beautiful—that life flows ("The Great Transparencies").

More personally in "What the Old Man Said," Sarton writes of her early mentor Lugné-Poë, founder of the Oeuvre Theatre in Paris. Throughout the poem the old man speaks—at ages sixty-five, sixty-seven, and finally seventy. Fighting against time and fashion that diminish the theater world he had known, Lugné-Poë—right or wrong—will not praise plays he finds inferior and will not himself despair at being the outsider of the world he had once centered. And in a purely occasional poem—"For Rosalind on Her Seventy-fifth Birthday"—Sarton honors advanced age. "Take your new-fangled beauties off the stage!" for the poet comes to praise "her splendor that has no age."

The poems upon the deaths of Virginia Woolf, Louise Bogan, Volta Hall (a psychiatrist), and Judith Matlack show how intensely Sarton has written of death when the loss is private and near. Several times in the 1930s Sarton met Virginia Woolf, whom she greatly admired. Sarton was lecturing in Chicago when she learned of Virginia Woolf's death, and the immediate shock eventually brought forth the poem, "Letter from Chicago. For Virginia Woolf." The poem begins, "Four years ago I met your death here, / Heard it where I had never been before." The juxtaposition of being in Chicago, a place she did not know well, and hearing painful news underscored the unsettling reaction. Sarton's passionate grief dominates, and the lapse of time—four years since Woolf's death—does not diminish her sense of loss. Briefly in the poem Sarton lets the focus shift too much to the speaker's emotions: "I wept wildly like a child / Who cannot give his present after all." But the force of the poem rests in Sarton's recognition of Woolf's death and the loss that death represents to the world of letters. The concluding line obliterates the conventional view of time and affirms the connection Sarton felt for Virginia Woolf; "I send you love forward into the past." ("Letter from Chicago. For Virginia Woolf" is one of three Sarton poems that Sandra Gilbert and Susan Gubar include in their recent *Norton Anthology of Literature by Women*.[13])

Sarton's "Elegy for Louise Bogan" (*A Durable Fire*, 1972) takes the surprising form of ten couplets, but the anticipated rhymes do not overpower the poem. By choosing "planet" rather than the expected "star" in the opening couplet, Sarton stresses Bogan's singularity as well as her remoteness. "The death of a poet hurts us terribly, / As if a planet sank down through the sky. / Just so she was remote, just so she shone, / Singular light has gone now she is gone." The details of Bogan's features reflect close observation—aqueous green eyes—as well as her violent heart, her innocent surprises, and especially her ironies "That kept her crystal clear and made us wise." Though the lament lacks restraint when Sarton cries, "Louise, Louise, why did you have to go / In this harsh time of wind and shrouding snow" and suffers from the obvious rhyme of "go / snow" as well as from the redundant "shrouding snow," the poem as a whole speaks deep friendship and

respect. Sarton knew well the emotional strain that dominated much
of Bogan's life and in a slant domestic image—"kneading a celestial
bread"—suggests the burdens under which Bogan lived and worked.
"Deprived, distraught, often despairing, / You kneaded a celestial
bread for sharing."[14] And certainly Sarton was among those who admired Louise Bogan's poems.

"Death of a Psychiatrist" (for Volta Hall) in *A Private Mythology* uses
the villanelle stanza in part 1 and then tercets, couplets, and quatrains.
The mixing of stanza forms, however, is not distracting, primarily
because Sarton writes a moving tribute to this remarkable doctor. (Hall
died of a heart attack.) The opening theme—"Now the long lucid
listening is done"—establishes the doctor/patient relationship and
shows Dr. Hall's talent as listener. The patient, so dependent upon his
listening, mourns his death as one mourns the death of a father. Part
2 expands the details of listening that touched and encouraged the
patients in their distress: "It was not listening alone, but hearing, /
For he remembered every crucial word / And gave one back oneself
because he heard. / Who listens so, does more than listen well. / He
goes down with his patient into Hell."

For Sarton, Dr. Hall's intent listening to a poem of hers was of
primary importance. He would ask that she "Read it again" and in that
"richest silence" that he could give, she knew the particular poem
would live. The concluding two lines end the tribute by praising the
skill of listening as the center of his therapeutic method. "Because he
cared, he heard; because he heard, / He lifted, shared, and healed,
without a word" (97–98). Several years after Volta Hall's death and
after the elegy had been published, members of Dr. Hall's family had
occasion to tell Sarton how deeply her poem had touched them.

On an even more personal level Sarton's poems for Judith Matlack
embody deep feeling. "A Light Left On" records the quiet intimacy of
their many years together—that "deepest world we share / And do not
talk about / But have to have, was there, / And by that light found
out" (*Selected Poems,* 50). Judith Matlack's last years were blighted by
Alzheimer's disease, and her debilitation was extreme as she lost connections with the present. News of her death ended the dehumanizing
suffering, and for Sarton it allowed the good memories to surface.
"Mourning to Do" (in the recent book of poems, *Letters from Maine,*
1984) gathers memories and permits what Sarton wisely calls happy
grieving. "So it is now the gentle waking to what was, / And what is

and will be as long as I am alive. / 'Happy Grieving,' someone said who knew— / Happy the dawn of memory and the sunrise." (Sarton has written a tribute, *Honey in the Hive,* 1988, a portrait of Judith Matlack privately published by Matlack's nephew, Timothy Matlack Warren.)

Nothing has ever affected Sarton as deeply as her mother's death. In 1939 Sarton wrote to S. S. Koteliansky to tell him that Mabel Sarton's mother, May's grandmother, had died. In reporting this event, Sarton anticipates the suffering she will endure when her own mother dies. "I think," she wrote to Koteliansky, "of K[atherine] M's[ansfield] letters when her mother died—and of waking up when I was [a] child sobbing because I had dreamed that mother was dead, with a sense of desolation that even her presence did nothing to help, because I knew it *would* happen some day" (Manuscript letter, 21 May [1939]).

The anxiety of the childhood dream was realized in November 1950 when Mabel Sarton died after a hard battle with cancer. Sarton wrote to William Theo Brown and her image—"the slow difficult uprooting"—suggests not only the agony of dying itself but also the altered world that death causes. "Mother died on Sat. very peacefully in her sleep—thank God it is over. The last three weeks were so awful and at the end one felt the slow difficult uprooting. . . . She was beautiful and herself to the end though literally wasted away, and after it was over I know I shall feel her radiant presence by my side" (Manuscript letter, 20 November 1950). Three poems in particular—"After Four Years," "An Observation," and "A Hard Death"—represent the most poignant statements about Mabel Sarton's death. Before it was collected into the volume, *In Time Like Air,* "After Four Years" had appeared in the *New York Herald Tribune* (26 February 1956) and in the March 1956 issue of the *Atlantic Monthly.* When *In Time Like Air* was published in 1958, Sarton included Vita Sackville-West among those to whom she sent a copy. In a clear (but not an especially pretty) hand Vita Sackville-West wrote a long reply from Sissinghurst Castle in Kent, commenting on the volume, noting that she especially liked "Where Dreams Begin," "Lady with a Falcon," and "Somersault." About the poem on Mabel Sarton's death, "After Four Years," Sackville-West wrote that she had known the poem for some time, having clipped it out of a magazine when it appeared (presumably in the *Atlantic Monthly*) and placing the poem in an album along with other clippings that she found drew her attention and merited saving. Vita Sackville-West's strained relation with her own mother contrasts sharply with the intimacy Mabel and May Sarton shared. It is interesting then that Sackville-West was so drawn to this poem where a daughter voices her "unnatural grief" over the mother's death and where her agony finally reaches acceptance and reconciliation. "And here lay down at last / Her long hard death, / And let her be in joy, be ash, not breath, / And let her gently go into the past, / Dear world, to rest at last." When Sarton published *A World of Light* (1976), that book included the five portraits already published in the *New Yorker*. In the portrait of Mabel Sarton she wrote, "When my mother died I felt relief for her . . . and relief for myself because I know that the worst thing that could ever happen to me has happened. Only my own death would ever take from me as much" (*WL,* 21).

Sarton has found it difficult to write about her mother's death and has remarked she was glad to come upon the gardening metaphor that made "An Observation" (*A Private Mythology,* 71) possible. "True gardeners," she begins, "cannot bear a glove / Between the sure touch and the tender root." She watches, and minds, as her mother's bare hands work the earth and bear the scars of that labor. Her example as true gardener is literal and metaphoric. Implicit in living and in gardening is the truth that one has to learn; the accumulation of experience is essential. The survivor must seize this truth: "we must be hard / To move among the tender with an open hand, / And to stay sensitive up to the end / Pay with some toughness for a gentle world."

Sarton wrote "A Hard Death" (*A Grain of Mustard Seed,* 1971) immediately after Mabel Sarton died, but did not publish it until some years afterwards. It is a poem she has sworn never to read in public, and when she attempted to do so during a recent taped interview, she lost control in the emotion the poem induced. Shocked by the indifferent care that hospital personnel extend to the dying, the speaker says, "'Is there compassion?'" a friend asks me / "'Does it exist in another country?'" The stark personal loss in death is simply rendered, and the flower image is central as it has been throughout the lives of both this mother and this daughter. "I saw my mother die and now I know / The spirit cannot be defended. It must go / Naked even of love at the very end. / 'Take the flowers away.'" The flowers must be taken away from one who throughout life "had been their friend." The intensity of the grief is matched by the intensity of May Sarton's love for her mother. She must now let the mother go, expressing in the last line the finality of death: "Only the living can be healed by love."[15]

The grief over Mabel Sarton's death fills letters that George Sarton

writes to his daughter in 1954. "Today is raining, raining. I wonder
how you have it in Ireland? It is a sad day for me, Mother's birthday;
she would have been 76, and I can not offer her any present" (Manuscript letter, 3 August 1954). And a few months later he writes, "Today is the anniversary of Mother's death four years ago. I wish I had
died at the same time" (Manuscript letter, 18 November 1954).

The extraordinary suffering that Mabel Sarton endured made George
Sarton's sudden death a relief and blessing. In the fullness of his powers
(he was en route to Logan Airport on his way to a lecture engagement)
he suffered a fatal heart attack. (He was able to return to his own house
before he died.) Sarton has described it as "a magnificent death," a
reaction some acquaintances found inapropos. She answers those who
criticize her apparent lack of grief in a poem, "Of Grief," where she
praises death that her father could die "in his splendid prime." Those
who find this reaction heartless have not known (Sarton writes in the
poem), have never witnessed a "slow death." Again, the supreme agony
of her mother's death surfaces: "My heart broke for my mother. / I
buried grief with her."

A second poem, "A Celebration for George Sarton" (*In Time Like
Air*, 1958), repeats the theme of relief and acceptance. The four ten-
line stanzas in rhyming couplets maintain a strong four-foot line that
keeps the restraint well. Through details of the life George Sarton
lived, his daughter remembers and reverses him—part of her accepting
of this father who had, in many ways, failed to cope with family life
and problems. His relentless scholarly work dominated his life and his
attention, but the poem lovingly recounts moments that are both
touching and endearing: "Loved donkeys, children, awkward ducks, /
Loved to retell old simple jokes." This scholar wrote letters until very
late so that neighbors who did not even know him knew his light; he
found comfort in an orange cat; and he worked, Sarton says as the poem
closes, "as poets work, for love."

Finally, without a trace of overreaction and in moving lines Sarton
writes "Burial." An old man digs a small pit and with a penknife forces
open the two boxes of ashes. And this ill-matched yet wonderfully
matched husband and wife, May Sarton's parents, are here reunited.
"My father and my mother gently laid / Into the earth and mingled
there for good." Those who watched saw the wind breathe upon the
ashes. The four people who stood and watched, "believing what they
could," bear witness to the scene and to this final union. "And that
was all: the bitterness of death / Lifted to air, laid in the earth" (*A
Durable Fire*, 61).

## Poems of the Garden

A 1988 interview series given over the Public Broadcasting System, "I'm Too Busy To Talk Now: Interviews with Artists over 70," included a talk with May Sarton. In the course of her remarks Sarton said she simply could not live without flowers. And she means the statement literally and symbolically. Flowers of the winter window box and of the spring and summer garden bring aesthetic pleasure; their presence within the garden patterns and within house arrangements brings delight. To Sarton, flowers are also the reminder of inevitable growth—its full cycle from the slightest bud to the full open blossom to faded and then falling petals and leaves. The human and natural patterns of birth, flourishing, and death are self-evident.

Three particular gardens have always been central to Sarton. First, the memories of Wondelgem in Belgium, where the young Mabel and George Sarton began their married life and where May Sarton lived her first few years. George Sarton's Uncle Arthur wrote a charming account of his visit to the young family, commenting especially on their garden. He found it "unique, relative to its small size" and called the house and garden open and light. The young Sartons were, he declared, "certainly in England and not at all in the stuffy antiquarian atmosphere of Ghent" (*IP,* 73).

The second garden is that of the Limbosch family, the Belgian business associates of Mabel Sarton and the close friends of them all. Here the garden provides the profusion of flowers, trees, vegetables, and animals that are gathered (Sarton notes in a poem called "The Garden of Childhood," *A Durable Fire,* 54) in "Chaotic splendor framed by a clipped lawn." Apple trees were close by arbors of roses and clematis; borders showed forth lupine, foxglove, lilies, and iris; animals marched about begging crumbs—Franz the Goose, a cock, a guinea hen, two ducks, a Persian cat. It was to this family, their house, and their garden that Sarton so often returned on many a trip to Europe. The details of this garden become "Emblems of all our summers and all our teas." Those summer hours exist most vividly in her memory, seen now she writes in an excellent image, as "an illuminated page. / The assiduous monk in his joy did not spare / Costly vermilion and gold, nor the rich sage." The intermingling of color, art, and labor links the growing garden and the rich illumination from the monk's hand.

The third garden is the annual one that Mabel Sarton always planted and a garden that May Sarton has replicated all her life. When she writes her journal *At Seventy,* Sarton answers those who charge that she is obsessed by the garden and its demands. One devotes time and energy to the garden, she says because both the gambler and the puritan within oneself are satisfied within the limitless expenditure and failure the garden requires and by its simple hard work and, one can add, the luck of the weather. Much of her poetry can be read as the annual cycle of the garden. "February Days" (*A Durable Fire*, 51) centers on "The long shadows of trees on snow," on light that now produces shadows of blue. The garden still lies dormant, but in the house a crimson cyclamen has opened wide, drunk on this February light. The rigor of the long New England winter discourages any hope of an early spring. "March in New England" (*A Durable Fire*, 53) details the icy grip and an atmosphere that delays thoughts of a flourishing garden. "All seems exhausted by its own withholding, / Its own withstanding. There is no unfolding / Even the new moon promises no better / Than a thin joke about much colder weather."

Many poems, of course, center on the spring days when the garden finally begins its renewal. There is, for instance, "Spring Song" (*The Lion and the Rose*, 67) where on a spring night the apple blossoms are full and white and with the morning have given way to an orchard green. "May Walk" (*A Durable Fire*, 23) catalogs the early trees in bloom while "Roses" carefully watches this flower's "rich brief day" as its *folded, enfolded,* compact world *unfolds* in full bloom. Sarton's poetry of the garden is not simply a response to the garden's aesthetic pleasure. The garden is a physical necessity of her work routine and thus a time of solitude and, as she calls it in "A Country Incident" (*A Private Mythology*, 77), a time of "haphazard meditation."

This poem chronicles a trivial narrative incident: a neighbor interrupts Sarton while she is planting bulbs and does not understand the total absorption this task can demand. Gardening is not casual diversion, but work converted into passionate play and, for Sarton, an activity she guards. She does so as, she reflects, her scholarly father had guarded his hours of reading and writing. "And, courteous in every other way, / Would not brook anything that kept him from / Those lively dialogues with man's whole past." So Sarton is unrepentant. Her irritation toward the neighbor who distracts her, who breaks the absorption, is real. She must ask this neighbor's indulgence because the act of serious gardening must not be thwarted. The full integration of garden and gardener is also conveyed in "A Flower-Arranging Summer" (*Cloud, Stone, Sun, Vine*) where Sarton questions a morning's activity and time: "Was this to waste it / In a long foolish flowery meditation?" The answer follows and shows the meditative self at work throughout the time spent with the flowers. "Within the floating world all is sensation. / And yet I see eternity's long wink / In these elusive games, and only there. / When I can so suspend myself to think / I seem suspended in undying air."[16] Summer's profusion gives way to late gardens of autumn where asters and unpruned roses abound, where pruning must soon dominate activity. And so the garden gives way at last to winter winds until the cycle begins again.

Throughout the garden poems[17] Sarton's imagery emphasizes the nourishing of the poet's self. "Pruning the Orchard" (*Halfway to Silence*, 1980), for example, correlates pruning the garden and asking the Muse to "pour strength into my pruning wrist / That I may cut the way toward open space." The garden poems frequently echo the joy and pleasure of love—the apple blossoms in "Spring Song" *(The Lion and the Rose)* are full and white upon the spring night and associated with a peaceful night of love. But the early doom that threatens this fruit is analogous to the disaster this love affair faces. "My love, my love, the fruit already knotted / After a single night."

Public gardens have also interested Sarton and have on occasion been the source for poems. "The Metaphysical Garden" grew from an autumn visit to Dumbarton Oaks, and within the poem Sarton traces the walk about the garden that two lovers make, seeing that their choice of path and progress takes on the meaning of their relationship as well as the literal journey. To contemplate such a garden, the poem argues, the pair must come out of it and return to ordinary life. They literally sit on "a homely wooden bench" and watch a solitary gardener go forth with a pruning hook. But the experience within the poem has been one of an "unbroken sunlit peace of knowing." For Sarton, the garden, public or her own, provides an essential pleasure, an essential part of daily routine whose influence goes far beyond the eye's pleasure.

## The Poems of Love

It is not surprising to find love poems the most prominent type throughout Sarton's work. Indeed, she distinguished one volume by simply declaring that it contained no love poems. Not all are successful, but many convey powerful emotion through images of seasonal cycles, flowers, movement of the sea and sea creatures, fields in harvest. Two early volumes—*Encounter in April* (1937) and *Inner Landscape* (1939)—and two much later volumes—*Cloud, Stone, Sun, Vine* (1961) and *A Durable Fire* (1972)—contain love poems in sonnet sequences. Indeed, the love poems that comprise the sequence, "A Divorce of Lovers" *(Cloud, Stone, Sun, Vine)*, are, as Henry Taylor has argued, among Sarton's "richest and most accomplished work."[18] In this sequence, as in many other individual poems, the gender of the lovers is not revealed and this information is not necessary to capture the detail of lived experience and of love.

Twenty sonnets comprise "A Divorce of Lovers." The title suggests both a legal and an emotional separation, a formal parting that insists on issues being properly settled. Sarton has said that she wrote these poems while she was on a lecture trip. Ill and running a high fever, she would be forced to get up in the night and write them down as lines literally flowed through her head. In his article Taylor traces the progress of the sequence through a series of strong paradoxes: speech and silence, splitting and healing, power as action and power as passivity.[19] These paradoxes do form a useful basis for examining the sequence.

In sonnet 1 Sarton introduces the central image, medical surgery, to discuss how Reason operates on Poetry. The extended image—one of her most effective poetic devices—establishes the tone of the difficult love affair. The speaker refers to *ether* and the need to *anaesthetize* the *wound*, to the *surgeon* who must crack apart the tight-clasped hand, and to the *scalpel* that must unknot love at the bone. The surgeon's name, we are told, is Reason and what we shall watch is how Reason *operates* on Poetry. This imagery sets up the entire sequence. On the one hand, Reason operates—i.e., makes an incision to correct a disorder. In this case, the intellect and control governed by Reason allow the poems to be written since distance from the experience has been gained. On the other hand, the *surgery* is only partially successful. The patient is not fully restored, but must bear scars—of the surgery itself and of the painful experience that has itself caused the wound. Whatever restoration might have been effected fails because the lovers irrevocably part. Sonnet 1 announces the divorce of these lovers: "Never will you and I meet face to face."

Sonnet 2 takes up an entirely different image, and again Sarton successfully extends the image throughout. The lovers' lives, like a rich "tapestry" has been started and "woven, stitch by stitch," bound together. The divorce requires now "unweaving." The tapestry of their love must be "separated stitch by stitch"; they must "snap the thread, cut, tear the bright thread out." They had been so fully woven together that the speaker declares the task of unweaving will not be finished until she dies. And the speaker laments the break before the whole design was finished. What could have been a full rich life together is lost and that fact, the speaker declares, is "your tragic epitaph, and mine."

Sonnet 3 continues the death imagery introduced with the epitaph—"One death's true death, and that is—not to care." In this sonnet the speaker and the lover are sharply distinct. The speaker's nightmare foreshadowed the ending, the divorce that now condemns "us to wake up alone." The lover is characterized as one who would "kill love and reason mystery" and the speaker insists, condemn "yourself to death, not me." The irreconcilable way of viewing continues in sonnet 4 where the speaker is baffled by the lover who insists on the divorce and who will "make your peace in such a ruthless fashion." The speaker cannot make the break with such ease.

Sonnet 5 presents the lovers' opposite reactions to this divorce where "Four rooted years [were] torn up without a qualm." The lover is characterized by her calm, her silence, her lack of feeling; the speaker by her small cries, her anguish. The lover, now associated with calculating poise, shocks the speaker by setting the limited scope this relationship now can have. "And we shall lunch, you say, that is our scope." This meager social and public meeting is to replace the intimacy of the four years of love. The distance now between the two is immense and the speaker describes that change ambiguously. "A living woman," the concluding three words, refers (as Taylor points out) to the speaker who is still alive but no longer loved and to the lover who is still alive but who has dismissed the speaker. "Between what we have lost and still might save / Lies, very quiet, what was once too human, / And lovely, and beloved, a living woman." Sonnet 6 continues to focus on the speaker's agony ("this one mortal wound") and on the lover's ability to move away from the relationship with relative ease ("And it is you who unmarry me"). Here there is full admission that the relationship had not been one of magical ease, for they had torn "every joy out of such pain." Other sonnets (8 and 9 particularly) show the speaker's disoriented state—like a circling airplane, like a homing pigeon whose instinct has run afoul. The speaker suffers the chaos of misdirection. Like other lost and wandering creatures, "now rocked and hurtled through the empty spaces, / We hang upon the hope that some thin radar / May light from deep within our darkened faces, / And tell us what to do, and where we are."

The center sonnet, the tenth, expresses a major theme Sarton has always held. The lover refuses to face the unpleasant aspects that cause the break—anger, fury, jealousy—and buries "childish hunger, childish greed." The speaker is right, Sarton would say, to "stand fast and face the animal." The necessity of letting feelings out and of facing the destructive demons with one's self are needful steps for growth. Suppression is simply suppression and delay.

This sonnet sequence documents much pain, but also much reflection on the inevitable failure many relationships are doomed to suffer. The lovers in this sequence had "met too late to know our meeting kind," and they had assumed that impossible task of changing the other: "Too late for me to educate your heart, / Too late for you to educate my mind." Finally in sonnet 14, after the speaker has tried in vain to understand the lover's motives, to reconcile the rupture, to recover the relationship, she turns inward. A major shift of focus comes as the speaker says, "let solitude begin." The turbulent and disconcerting weather that had dominated earlier sonnets now (in sonnet 15) becomes a lull of wind and rain and skies that "move in slow motion overhead." Renewal begins (in sonnet 16) with a return of the domestic routine in "this house where the long silences restore / The essence and to time its real dimension." The solitude increases the loss—"Though this was time that we had planned to spend / Together, circled on the calendars"—but the solitude also begins to settle the change. Intimacy and physical presence are no longer possible; they must remain apart, yet still connected: "You hold me in your heart, as I hold you."

The last four sonnets in the sequence, "A Divorce of Lovers," focus on the speaker's strength and restoration. Renewed courage compensates for the agony she has suffered, and the speaker welcomes back "my wandering soul / Into these regions of the strange transcendence, / And find myself again, alive and whole" (in sonnet 17). And for the speaker—as for Sarton—the restoration means that she is once again made "an instrument for song." Now it is Poetry that will "pour through me your ruthless word / As strong as once was love that used me hard" (in sonnet 19). The concluding sonnet invokes silence and declares that all the illusions must be let go. There has been no easy way to give up what had gone between them, no avoiding pain and suffering. Sarton's primary emphasis in the entire sequence comes in sonnet 20 when she says, "Against our will now we are forced to grow / And push out from all safety into song." On each side lies truth and

illusion, love and regret. The great longing for this love must, however, be let go.

Sarton seldom includes sensuous detail, but a slight bit appears in
"After All These Years" when she writes, "I kiss small naked ears / And
stroke a marble cheek." Rarely do we learn what the lovers' physical
appearance is—fair or dark, blue eyes or brown, tall or short. Sarton's
interest lies in the experience of the love relation itself and what the
engagement brings at the time it occurs and what that engagement
means to the individuals once the affair ends.

The sheer impulse of love cannot be denied nor fully held in check.
For example, the ninth sonnet in the *Inner Landscape* sequence asks how
can one "deny the passion that is bound in you" or bind the "quicksil-
ver that courses through the blood." The quickening of deep emotion
may lead to a passionate connection or it may lead (as in "Augenblink")
to a brief but bold instant—out of five hundred faces there will be an
instant recognition with *one*. The bond is immediate and may be love
or merely a flash of recognition. The poem ephasizes tht one should
seize the experience—"give and take an honest glance." Sarton believes
that experiences must be seized and lived fully, not denied and by-
passed. She pursues this theme in her remarks for the film, *May Sarton:
A World of Light*. People, she says, fear and dread death bcause they
have not lived their lives, have not done the unexpected or the daring.
They are suddenly brought up short and realize that they have not
*really* lived.

Throughout these many love poems Sarton repeats with a convincing
insistence the same primary points. Love in its earliest stages is madness and one is powerless to stop an inevitable experience—that easy
and bright weather. But most of the poems take up the experience of
love after that initial burst of passion, after the madness surrounding
the experience of falling in love. Serious love, these poems show, is
never simple or casual. It exacts a price because relationships are difficult to maintain. Jealousy, rage, infidelity are constant threats. Two
poems in particular use images that indicate how difficult the relationship is to maintain and foster. "Love" in *Halfway to Silence* portrays the
relation as "Fragile as a spider's web / Hanging in space / Between tall
grasses." The intricate and beautiful web is whole, but the slightest
thing—even a dog passing by—can shatter that spun web. And so,
Sarton says, it is with love. The poem ends with the relentless spider,
that patient weaver, who never stops repairing and reweaving the web.

It is, the poet says, no doubt hunger and hope that keep the spider and the human lover at their tasks. In "Of Mollusks" (*Halfway to Silence*) Sarton renders lover locked—like the shelled mollusk—in a cold, impenetrable impasse. No instrument of force but only the rising tide and its slow progress will effect a change. Angry lovers cannot easily be reconciled but, like the mollusks, must "eat, rest, be nourished on the tide." For the lovers, that tide must be *love*.

Sarton's poems explore the far-reaching effects of love. More than ecstasy, she writes of suffering, silence, solitude, communion, wisdom, partings, farewells, and death when she writes poems about love. Unless the blazing passion becomes the enduring flame of love, no lasting experience occurs. The loss of supreme passion is compensated for by the deep and enduring growth of love. Sonnet 11 in "The Autumn Sonnets" uses the extended image of the fire and the proper firewood to make this point. The details are familiar to anyone dependent on a good and steady fire that will not fail in winter's storm. No maker of fires chooses the "resinous pine" that bursts fast to flame and is quickly consumed. One chooses instead the slower and stronger "heart of oak" to produce "a durable fire." The analogy extends throughout the sonnet, and Sarton takes a commonplace image—the flame of love—and turns it into an excellent sonnet:

> For steadfast flame wood must be seasoned,
> And if love can be trusted to last out,
> Then it must first be disciplined and reasoned
> To take all weathers, absences, and doubt.
> No resinous pine for this, but the hard oak
> Slow to catch fire, would see us through a year.
> We learned to temper words before we spoke,
> To force the furies back, learned to forbear,
> In silence to wait out erratic storm,
> And bury tumult when we were apart.
> The fires were banked to keep a winter warm
> With heart of oak instead of resinous heart,
> And in this testing year beyond desire
> Began to move toward durable fire.
>
> (*A Durable Fire*, 47)

The occasion of love brings at the very beginning the threat of parting, of metaphoric death. The lovers in "Encounter in April" (a series of five sonnets) may beautifully come together like two deer and be beguiled by each other's grace but they also recognize that "no spring can be eternal, nor can this." Using two distinctly different sources of imagery—a detail of nature and an object of art—Sarton drives home the point: leave-taking accompanies the very beginning of love:

> You who are now my tropic and my south
> Will have turned cold before the robins settle—
>
> > (7)
>
> . . . . . . . . . . . . . . . . . . . . . . . . . . . . . . . . . . .
> Two Dresden figures ignorant of pain
> Her fan unchipped, still bright his blue cockade,
> The lady exquisite, the gallant swain—
> We said farewell after the escapade.
>
> > (9)

In "Mal du Départ" one lover goes away and leaves behind a death-like atmosphere. The house is now "the strange chilling tomb"; the lover's gift, a bouquet of tulips, has turned "brown at the tips"; the heart fire has gone to ashes; and "absence infects the air." The speaker needs "a healing sacrament" to be restored and for the moment assumes the role of invalid. The pain of lost love is deathlike. The speaker "can hardly draw / A solitary breath / That does not hurt me like a little death." In a very early poem Sarton uses the death image in a stanza that sounds almost like Emily Dickinson, both in tone and substance, if not in slant rhyme:

> This is the crisp despair
> Lying close to the marrow,
> Fallen out of the air
> Like frost on the narrow
> Bone of a shot sparrow.
> (*Encounter in April,* 3)

In spite of pain, the speaker gains through the suffering. Ideally, silent communion comes. Lovers pass beyond speech into what Sarton calls "rich silence" that is "beyond speech, outside reason" ("Time for Rich Silence"). Clearly, Sarton herself seems usually to be the speaker, the sufferer in these poems. As she emerges from love affairs, she persistently finds solace in her house and its routine (in Nelson and now in York) and in her work. Often the poems themselves declare that the pain of the broken affair has indeed pushed her into poetry. The irony

of the suffering exists in the translation of suffering—consistently for
Sarton—into poetry.

In the sonnet sequences and in many single poems Sarton writes of
love, usually of the consequences that document the ending of love
affairs, the battles and agonies of lost love, and the process of restoration. Never does she deny the possibility of a state of full love and
compatibility. When it does occur, it is like music's harmony: "We
enter the evening as we enter a quartet / Listening again for its particular note" ("Evening Music"). In reality, however, the poems deal more
with agony, suffering, pain—more consequences that speak of love
lost.

The love poems in her recent volume, *Letters from Maine* (1984),
make a bold demand that love late in life is to be acknowledged. It is
"a brief amazing union" that "The November Muse" brought—did
"give me wisdom and laughter, also clarity" (Letter 2). The speaker
looks at the unlikely circumstance for a love to flourish and says, "How
for that matter / Did it all happen when we met? / Time telescoped,
years cast away." Most of all, the two were indeed "lifted beyond age"
(Letter 4). But the illusions do not hold, and the lover says by telephone and from a great distance, "Perhaps we should never meet
again." The speaker's reaction in letter 8 echoes a line from Louise
Bogan that Sarton has known for many years. Bogan's advice to Sarton
was often that she should confront life less intensely, confront it more
naturally "as the grass grows on the weirs." The speaker in these poems
has not taken love or poetry casually and says she is unable "to take
love lightly as the grass / Grows on the weirs." Once again, solitude
and pain emerge in poetry—"Everything stops but the poem"—and
Sarton brings the speaker at the close of *Letters from Maine* to a voice
that is strong, confident, self-assured. The religious imagery at the end
weakens the group of poems somewhat, and they do not display the
power of "The Autumn Sonnets" or "A Divorce of Lovers." Still, Sarton's claim for love in old age is bold and a claim she confidently
makes. It is a theme that several of her novels have also argued and
explored.

In the early volume, *Encounter in April*, fifteen sonnets show that
Sarton's most important convictions about love and love poetry have
been consistently embodied in her verse, early and late. However, this
early sequence is of interest because she suggests in sonnet 2 that the
lovers are man and woman (rather than a lesbian relationship), and here

the woman speaks, asking that the overture that will bring on love-making be postponed. She speaks, "Don't touch. O let me be / A little while this woman with a name / Before I lose it for eternity." She would keep herself and her lover "ourselves instead of man and woman." This insistence of individuality, of acknowledging the *self* as *self*, remains central to Sarton's vision—particularly that a woman maintain her *self*. Love threatens that self, creating the pair and perhaps losing the individual. In sonnet 2 the woman asks that each of the two "Keep for a moment each his single heart / Before we reach the immemorial common / Place of lovers in the dream of time, / And merge into a rhythm and each other."

Sonnet 14 with its allusion to particular and acid fruits (persimmons, pomegranate juice, crabapple, late plum) introduces the inevitable separation of lovers. Sarton here embodies a dual theme central to much of her work: one is nourished by loneliness but dependent on the lover's presence for happiness. "I have been nourished by this loneliness," the speaker says as the sonnet begins. Yet the concluding lines shift the imagery from nourishment to the act of starving. Fulfillment can come only with the lover's presence. The heart, the speaker declares, would starve "If it were held another hour apart / From that food which alone can comfort it— / I am come home to you, for at the end / I find I cannot live without you, friend."

As we have seen in the late poems, in the novels, and especially in the journals, age brings a decided change in the individual and, for Sarton, the benign state of solitude replaces the difficulty loneliness presents. Women, she would say, become less dependent upon love as they are more sustained and nourished by solitude.

## Women's Poems

Much of Sarton's poetry centers on women—herstory. There are, for examples, poems directly about famous women—Eleonora Duse, Virginia Woolf, Elizabeth Bowen—declaring the public presence of each and celebrating them as women and as artists. Very early, Sarton was struck with the power of Georgia O'Keeffe and praises the great strength of O'Keeffe's flower paintings in "Portrait of One Person as by Georgia O'Keeffe." This 1937 poem shows Sarton working in a very tight form and praising O'Keeffe before it was commonplace to do so. Three poems, perhaps, will serve to show the extreme emphases Sarton has always placed on "women's poems": "She Shall Be Called Woman"

(*Encounter in April*, 1937), "My Sisters, O My Sisters" (*The Lion and the Rose*, 1948), and "Gestalt at Sixty" (*A Durable Fire*, 1972). It is important to notice at the outset, that her poems about women and women's discovery of themselves began very early, as the dates of these poetry collections indicate. The ten-part "She Shall Be Called Woman" (in *Encounter in April*) is a bold poem celebrating Eve. She discovers her body without quite knowing what it is and then experiences full sexual desire, violation, response, and finally pleasure. Although there are lapses in diction and imagery (Eve's breasts stand "straightly / out from her chest"), the poem is important for *woman* as woman to celebrate the sensuousness of her own body, to discover and accept her sexual identity.

"My Sisters, O My Sisters" (one of the three poems Gilbert and Gubar include in their *Norton Anthology*) bears an epigraph from Anna de Noailles: "Nous qui voulions poser, image ineffaceable / Comme un delta divin notre main sur le sable." The irony—leaving one's ineffaceable image like a handprint in the sand—is self-evident. The poem invokes important women from the past—Dorothy Wordsworth, Dickinson, Rossetti, George Sand, George Eliot, Madame de Staël, Madame de Sevigne, Sappho—to link their history to contemporary women who share the same need of expression and power. In the self-portrait film, *A World of Light*, Sarton reads this poem, but only part 1. This cut version may account for some who have read "My Sisters" as a radical lesbian poem. It is nothing of the sort, as a careful reading of the whole poem shows. Indeed, the poem insists that only by building inward and by renouncing passion did any of these famous women succeed: "Only in the extremity of spirit and flesh / And in renouncing passion did Sappho come to bless."

The poem declares that women writers—women artists in general—are strange monsters who must become more human, must get to that place where the poet becomes woman and flourishes in feminine power. Part 2 celebrates the female body (echoing the much earlier "She Shall Be Called Woman") and presents woman as the comforter of man, the nourisher of children. She must maintain the balance between being the gentle dove, the wily serpent. Part 3 argues that women have the double heritage—Eve, the giver of knowledge and the nourisher; Mary, the shield, the healer, the Mother. This double heritage imposes a delicate balance; chaos results when the balance collapses and woman becomes then the destroyer. Sarton names some of the demands many women have had to assume. Many have been obliged to mother their

husbands; many have loved an only son "as a lover loves." The difficulty of living and of maintaining a proper balance of roles is the problem. How many women, Sarton asks,

> yield up their true power
> Out of weakness, the moment of passion
> Betrayed by years of confused living—
> For it is surely a lifetime work,
> This learning to be a woman.
> Until at the end what is clear
> Is the marvelous skill to make
> Life grow in all its forms.
>                    (In *The Lion and the Rose*, 60)

The poem concludes with the renunciation theme again. If women
are to find themselves, they must "ask men's greatness back from men,
/ Until we make the fertile god our own, / And giving up our lives,
receive his own." Women readers in the eighties must find many aspects of the poem out of tune for the times. However, I think the poem
mirrors a fundamental premise for Sarton: the suggestion that androgyny is the desirable state. The last line—"And giving up our life,
receive his own"—is intolerable if it means women give up all individuality, all sense of self in the service of men. If, instead, it can be read
as an avenue to androgyny where one individual accepts and welcomes
within herself the male and female impulses, then an ideal wholeness
results. Thus, dealing with the entire poem suggests not a singular
capitulation to men, but argues instead that women deal with the
"double river" of their natures and accord man his power too. Through
the years Sarton has continually resisted the militant gestures of fem-
inists and has insisted that—without losing themselves—women must
not wage battle with men, but must live and work harmoniously with
them.

"Gestalt at Sixty" *(A Durable Fire)* is one of Sarton's most personal
and most appealing poems. As she turns sixty and reflects upon the
ten years of living alone in her renovated farmhouse in Nelson, New
Hampshire, Sarton writes of solitude, pain, endurance, change. She
does not indulge any one of her many roles—poet, woman, lover—but
finds all roles demanding and all offering challenge. The independent
woman living alone[20] is the source of envy for many women who have
found their identity solely as the comforter of men, the nourisher of

children. Sarton, however, insists that solitude is risky, filled with dangers: "I can tell you that solitude / Is not all exaltation, inner space / Where the soul breathes and work can be done. / Solitude exposes the nerves, / Raises up ghosts." The anguish that comes as one lives alone is real and must be endured. For Sarton, the garden is the key to enduring: "I worked out angush in a garden / Without the flowers, / The shadow of trees on snow, their punctuation, / I might not have survived." The poem leads to major concerns, primarily the acceptance of change that "is always in the making / . . . If one can be patient"; of learning to trust oneself; and most important, of learning to trust death. Sarton ends this poem with a four-line benedictionlike coda that does not enhance the poem. In the self-portrait film she omits this coda when she reads the poem, suggesting that she herself does not always find it apropos.

Throughout her volumes of poetry Sarton devotes much space to women, women's lives, women's concerns. Alicia Ostriker, writing about women and myth poems, cites Sarton's "The Muse as Medusa" as a poem illustrating female experience. These female experiences reflected in women's poems allow the poet to retrieve "images of what women have collectively and historically suffered; in some cases they are instructions for survival." In "The Muse as Medusa" Sarton turns the Medusa around and discovers her own face, an image she must now explore. In making this gesture, Ostriker suggests, women will "gain knowledge of myth's inner meanings" and their own as well."[21]

Many of Sarton's poems are personal and expose details we readily can verify in her own life. Many, however, transcend the merely personal and speak to and for women of many generations. "The Geese" in *Halfway to Silence* is such a poem. Sarton uses the image of the annual progress of wild geese who, in a long wavering line, make their appointed journey south. She juxtaposes this scene with a woman alone who sees and hears the geese and is smitten with unexplained loneliness:

> It happens every year
> And every year some woman
> Haunted by loss and fear
> Must take it as an omen,
>
> Must shiver as she stands
> Watching the wild geese go,

> With sudden empty hands
> Before the cruel snow.
>
> Some woman every year
> Must catch her breath and weep
> With so much wildness near
> At all she cannot keep.[22]

Even the meter and rhyme speak for many a woman who instantly responds to the motion and direction of the departing geese and can only weep for that expressive wild side that she herself can not follow or, the reader infers, express.

During many of the long years that Louise Bogan was poetry critic for the *New Yorker,* she often saw May Sarton and certainly was aware of her work. One of Sarton's bitter disappointments remains the absence of decisive public recognition by Bogan in the pages of the *New Yorker.* Manuscript lettes show that Bogan carefully reserved expressing judgment and would not write a review for friendship's sake. These letters indicate Bogan felt that often Sarton's poetry did not go deep enough into primary emotions. The frequently quoted charge—Bogan said that Sarton "kept the hell out" of her poems—is an important point. Certainly, dozens of Sarton's poems do boldly deal with primary emotions—rage, frustration, grief, despair. Bogan said that the primary emotions were crucial to lyric poetry, and she felt that Sarton did not carry these emotions to their fullest extent. But few women poets have been able—especially in lyric verse—to plunder the frightening realms of the subconscious and to push emotions to their limit as did Louise Bogan. "The Daemon," "The Furies," "Psychiatrist's Song," and especially "Kept" take the reader into the lives of women with devastating exposure and, as Elizabeth Frank points out in her biography of Bogan, with "imaginative sympathy."

William Drake, in his study of women's poetry in America from 1914 to 1945, sees Sarton's poetry as "a kind of watershed in women's poetry in its deliberate avoidance of indirection and artistic game-playing in order to overcome the incapacitating effects of gender delimitation."[23] When Drake says that Bogan's refusal to engage in a passionate relationship with Sarton "recreated with May Sarton the tragedy of separation from her own mother,"[24] he perhaps overstates the point. No experience ever matched the one between May Sarton and her remarkable mother. To be sure, Sarton felt betrayed in the experience with Bogan, but her life as poet has continued and the disappointment at Bogan's hand did not silence her.

As Drake argues, Sarton is a harbinger of a new generation of poets from those who flourished between the wars and stands firm in the generation that challenged male ascendency. If in the late forties male poets tended to write poems of the avant garde, Louise Bogan and May Sarton flourished after 1945 and wrote primarily lyric verse. In doing so, they continued the work of many female poets who flourished before them—Sara Teasdale, Eleanor Wylie, Edna St. Vincent Millay. The preference for the lyric poem has remained constant for Sarton and in that form she has done some of her best work. And while she has not tolerated being dominated by male influence, she has steadily argued that great combat is not the answer. Sarton *always* knew that she was a poet, and it is to this art form that she has given her greatest energy.

# Chapter Five
# "It's been a long hard struggle"

May Sarton's history is rich and intricately layered, having its roots in her European background[1] and giving her a permanent feeling of exile in America, a feeling her mother deeply shared. Sarton's sense of divided allegiance is a far more important theme in her work than is generally recognized simply because many readers identify her with the American scene—her house in Nelson, New Hampshire (detailed in *Plant Dreaming Deep*), and now her home in York, Maine (detailed in *The House by the Sea*). Nevertheless, the sense of exile does run deep and has pushed Sarton to contemplate and embrace solitude and to identify with nature itself. There is, she declares, harmony in every tree, and the whole cycle of the earth's greening process is impartial, available to those who will observe it since it crosses territory at will and proceeds in its own course uncontrolled, uninterrupted. Sarton has indeed loved the American landscape, but she declares in her poem "From All Our Journeys" (*Cloud, Stone, Sun, Vine*) that "no continent can hold our whole allegiance." For Sarton, the cycles of the seasons and solitude have been and do remain the constants.

Her work itself provides a social history that is significant, especially in women's lives whether the fictional setting is Europe or America. Elaine Showalter points out that while our cultural anthropology and social history may possibly furnish the vocabulary "of women's cultural situation," she warns feminist critics that the concept must be used "in relation to what women actually write, not in relation to a theoretical, political, metaphoric, or visionary ideal of what women ought to write."[2] May Sarton's combination has been her persistence in keeping on with what she does well, with writing primarily of women who can and do face and welcome their extraordinary feelings, their independent manner of living, their solitude—hardly the "ideal vision of what women ought to write."

Sarton has, in a way, given a limited social history of women's lives after World War I. Her characters are almost always middle-class, educated, interested in the arts, reasonably alert to civic concerns. Al-

most all of her women characters are single by choice or have endured
a stressful marriage. The marriage usually has not let the woman develop intellectually or artistically unless she has forced the issue and
moved forward in spite of her husband or circumstances. The history
of these women involves their sense of place—their home or their business, the circle of friends with whom they spend time. Most important
in the lives of these women is the relationship (especially the conversations) they have with their closest women friends. Here their real
story is told, often the story their husbands and children never hear.

Except for *Mrs. Stevens Hears the Mermaids Singing,* Sarton seldom
explicitly introduces the subject of homosexuality in her fiction, but
the subject is one that she neither denies nor avoids. She considers that
as a hardworking and serious writer, as a person deeply committed to
fairness and responsibility, she is not to be labeled. The social history
she writes of and indeed lives has led her to explore women's lives,
especially the power and the fact of passion in women's relationships.
She also affirms that some of these relationships are lesbian ones. This
candor allows the raw nerve endings to be exposed, and capable of
"unladylike" behavior, her women characters display rage, depression,
despair, passion, and love. Sarton is fond of repeating Yeats's statement
that there is more risk—more enterprise—in going naked, and many
times she insists that her characters metaphorically do just that. The
social history records that characters do take risks and, very often for
the woman, that risk is claiming her place within the marriage or in
seeking a divorce. As we continue to discover what Showalter calls "the
evolution and laws of a female literary tradition,"[3] we will continue to
draw upon May Sarton's work as well as her life. Her forthrightness in
portraying women characters means these women finally do not suc-
cumb to men's power nor are they molded and changed as men would
have them be.[4] They appear, as Dora did to Freud, aberrant and yet
many of them—once they take charge of their lives—are independent
and strong.

Louise Bogan's poem "Evening in the Sanitarium" gives an excellent
picture of women who fail to live up to the images expected of them,
who fail to perform their domestic tasks. Now these women are in the
sanitarium where some have been helped and will, perchance, be nearly
well always but never, Bogan implies, altogether well. They knit (on
bone needles because they are safe and steel ones are not), they stare,
they stop drinking, and one even returns to her routine life but a life
controlled by her husband. Each evening she will meet his 5:45 train.

All these women are stifled and obedient, women who have been "denied their emotional and physical freedom, and condemned to pointless lives in stultifying gender roles."[5] The women in Bogan's poem contrast with many of the women in Sarton's novels and poems who are not sent off by husbands and sons and fathers to be made nearly well in a sanitarium. Instead, many of them go into business, leave their husbands, or come to terms with life and remain within the bonds of marriage, but not so much the victim as the partner.

Taken as a whole, Sarton's work constitutes a serious body of writing that spans over fifty years of active publishing. Her journals record the frustration and bitterness she has suffered from a lack of serious critical attention (perhaps too often she records this regret). While she has on occasion been singularly unlucky at the hands of unsympathetic reviewers, she has never given up. Year after year she has kept at the work, even from time to time pointing out when her published work could have been better. And all this while, she has been a thoroughly self-supporting writer, with relatively few teaching posts to supplement her income. A 1966 letter to Louise Bogan epitomizes the struggle that has followed Sarton's professional life. The letter catalogs the major issues: Sarton's recurring depression, the longed-for recognition, the unfair treatment, the admission of limited success, and the insistence that her work (especially the lyric poetry) is unfashionable:

I wake up with joy in the morning and this in itself is so new after months of really severe depression, anxiety and exhaustion that I can hardly believe it. I am very cross with the *Times* for not having reviewed Mythology [*A Private Mythology*]—somehow I felt they owed me a break after giving the Selected [*Cloud, Stone, Sun, Vine*] to Shapiro.[6] But one of the things I have been battling through is an attempt to simply write off ambition once and for all. Just *give up* and be happily and fruitfully my unfashionable, unsuccessful yet productive self. Let the bones shine in the dark after I am dead. For now, it does not matter. It has been a hard stance for me to achieve but I think I am there at last. It was the last devil I had to conquer. For I now intend to have about twenty years of happy work, and not to worry as they say. (16 September 1966)

Sarton has had more than twenty years of happy work since that letter and continues to produce; however, she has not entirely conquered the regret over the limited attention. What she has done is to stay with the view she holds for her work. Time and again in interviews May Sarton has said that she writes novels and poems to find out what she is really thinking. She has not written, she adds, to *tell* people things but to convey her own vision of life. For her, that vision is to have her work, as a whole, judged as idealistic and humanistic. To do so, she has followed her impulse to go very deep into the self, to push feelings into words, to introduce the issues that have guided her own life. The work contains no physical violence from one person to another, and though it centers on feeling and often on passion, few passages can be described as erotic. And the publication of *Mrs. Stevens Hears the Mermaids Singing* notwithstanding, Sarton should not be labeled a lesbian writer. Her social experience and her work are inclusive; that is, her view includes those relationships and modes of living that are genuine and honest, that allow a person to grow and develop and to be a happy, productive individual. She has by no means centered her subject matter or her themes on lesbian issues any more than Virginia Woolf did just because she published *Orlando.* Further, as I noted earlier, Sarton has not been sympathetic to feminist groups or to political confrontations that exist for their own sake.

In 1964 May Sarton spent part of the winter at Yaddo. From that retreat for writers, she wrote to her old friend, Basil de Selincourt, expressing her intense discouragement over her work in progress and, at age fifty-two, making a perceptive assessment of her talent both as novelist and as poet. What she identifies as her primary weakness as a novelist (lacking a social background) is not, I think, so much the point. The novels, as a whole, suffer because the energy in most of them goes into arguing an issue rather than in the development of characters and their lives. Characters are more voices for the issues, albeit most of those issues are significant and many of the characters interesting and appealing.

Sarton does, I think, precisely identify the weakness in her poetry— she has avowed dependence on a muse that has been literal and has so often made the poem dependent on a person and a place. Sarton here has the confidence and honesty to call her talent "a minor gift" that she worked a lifetime to develop and she has been diligent to use it as well as she can. One cannot ask more of the writer. Her words to de Selincourt make her point and assessment with candor and grace.

After ten months' work on a novel [probably *Mrs. Stevens*] Sarton fears it may be a "dud," fears that she may be written out:

I am, there is no doubt about it, *old-fashioned.* It came as a shock, for instance, when a young writer here [Yaddo] had never heard of Elizabeth Bowen who

was a shining star 20 years ago—I had at best a minor gift which I worked
very hard to perfect. I am not ashamed of the results. They are the best I had
in me and one does not create one's talent.

But as a novelist what I have lacked is a social background. The understanding and feeling were there, but the substance was lacking. I was European yet
not really, as we left there when I was so young. My parents were hermits etc.
I did not even share the usual American experience of going to college. It is
possible that this vein is written out—and I have said my say, my little say.

As a poet, I am quite disappointed in myself also. Too much has depended
on the conjunction of a person and a place, on Aphrodite rising from the
waves. (Manuscript letter, 26 November 1964)

Her life began in a household dedicated to scholarly work where the
joy of music, flowers, conversation were valued, in many ways, a world
to envy. And it has been a life dedicated to art, to producing works of
art. "What a masterpiece *Out of Africa* is," Sarton writes, "the perfect
example of what makes a work of art, experience distilled, sometimes
even distorted, so that truth transcends fact" (*S,* 267). That state, when
truth transcends fact, has been Sarton's intent throughout her life and
work. On the large desk in one room at Wild Knoll is a striking photograph of Isak Dinesen—that angular face, those sharp eyes looking
out at the viewer with rapt conviction. The photograph itself suggests
the truth transcending fact in Dinesen's remarkable life. May Sarton
doubtless sees this photograph daily, certainly has absorbed its presence
into her routine. That photograph serves perhaps to symbolize generations of women who were and are artists, who remain firm in their
artistic vision in spite of fashion and difficulty, who persevere to keep
their talent alive and producing. No one of her generation has done so
with more vigor and with more conviction than has May Sarton. One
*does not* create one's own talent, but each is responsible for developing
and exploiting her talent to its fullest life. Sarton has done so for over
half a century. It has, she says herself, been a long hard struggle, but
her work is there, her bones already shine.

## *Appendix*
# Editor to Author, Swenson and Sarton

The Sarton Papers in the Berg Collections contain seven typed auto-graph letters from May Sarton's editor, Eric Swenson, concerning the novel, *Mrs. Stevens Hears the Mermaids Singing.* Throughout these let-ters, all but one of which are here included entire, Swenson is enthu-siastic about the novel, and his editorial suggestions are to tighten, sharpen, focus, not make substantive changes either in form or con-tent, after Sarton had edited and revised the first draft. Indeed, Sarton herself was far more concerned about the less-than-traditional form than Swenson was; he immediately calls the manuscript a "novel" and insists that any other designation of form be avoided. Further, Swenson warns Sarton that the subject matter may cause some of her loyal read-ers to desert, but this warning is made to prepare her for this possible event, not at all to question the publication of the book.

Swenson's letters demonstrate the excellent rapport he and May Sar-ton enjoyed at that time and have continued to enjoy to the present day. His positive response to *Mrs. Stevens Hears the Mermaids Singing* is important to show the editor-to-author relationship, and the letters here presented are all the more important since Sarton's English agent (Patience Ross) and her American agent (Diarmuid Russell) were not at all enthusiastic about this novel. In a letter to her artist friend Wil-liam Theo Brown, Sarton transcribed Russell's reservations and her re-sponse to him. Russell's reservations centered on the book being "static" and "conversational" and far more an analysis of love and of the nature of the poetic process than a novel of people vitally engaged in life and complicated activities. Russell pointed out to Sarton that all of her previous novels presented characters who were fully engaged in active and lively processes, who fully showed forth their own society. Such a substantial base, Russell felt, was not present in *Mrs. Stevens;* although he sent his reservations with some reluctance, he sent them nevertheless.

Certainly Russell was right. The novel is static and conversational, and it does not fully engage the characters in an active and complicated plot that is centered within a present time and within a society that informs and engages characters and readers. What the novel does accomplish, however, is an internal recollection of a remarkable woman, lately come to fame and secure now to remember the past with complete candor. And the novel does indeed explore the nature of love, the sources of poetry—interesting subject matter for most readers. Further, the details in Swenson's letters suggest that a manuscript study of *Mrs. Stevens Hears the Mermaids Singing* would be useful.

I have included May Sarton's 25 May 1964 response to Swenson's letter of 8 May 1964 and her letter of 4 December 1964 because the two letters show the editor-to-author working relationship of Sarton and Swenson.

8 May 1964

Dear May,

First of all let me say that I like what you are trying to do immensely. It is a terribly important reason to write a novel. Second, I like the elements you have chosen as your means. Third, I think there will be many other people who will like it, when you have it right. This may well be the most important book you have written.

Fourth, my admiration for the quality of your self-criticism and self-editing is at an all-time high. Your letter seemed to me to go into the heart of the matter. This is particularly true when you said that you thought that what you have now is a schematization of what now must be written. In other words, the episodes, I think, must be given greater length. This is particularly true of Hilary's marriage, but I think it is also true of all the episodes.

For example Willa. In a sense you have cheated on her particularly. At the risk of sounding Bread-Loafish, I feel you have resorted to telling, not showing. See p. 48 and p. 51, and think what has been left out. It may well be that with these existing episodes written in full and from the inside point of view so that the reader can experience them fully, you have the whole book. I can't know that for sure, because I don't know what the remaining episodes are to be like.

I think you are right to have Hilary an old woman. There is only one thing that bothers me about her. She is presented as a very strong person, and yet in her story she merely reacts to strong people. If she really had been as powerful as she now seems in her old age, wouldn't she have had a somewhat similar effect on others?

About the beginning. I think you were right, on the telephone. I think it should plunge right in with Hilary and then bring the interviewers on stage. As it now is, the book comes [to] real life only when she arrives on the scene.

Peter bothers me a bit. He sounds sometimes lightweight and flip, even impertinent. Almost as soon as he meets Hilary this begins. Of course he must ask searching questions, but he seems purposelessly sarcastic at times. This may be a misreading of my own, but there it is.

Carol Houck has brought up a question which I had not thought of. She wonders whether the Willa and the Madelaine episodes should follow each other and whether or not one of the men should be in between perhaps Luc (a wonderful creation by the way). As I say, this hasn't occurred to me, but Carol may be right.

That is about it. The main thought is one you have already had, which is that these episodes have got to be expanded [so] that the reader can live them out—to experience "the peak experience." Whether or not the book should go on beyond the potential material already in it, I can't say, but I am intrigued by your little clue concerning the Finnish boy.

There it is, May. I think you have begun to work a major vein.

P.S. I am off to Paris for two days and then to London for two weeks, or so. I shall get in touch with you when I return.

25 May 1964

Dear Eric,

I am a little vague as to when you get back—trust all went well. Paris must have been beautiful at this season despite the racket—it has become so noisy.

Your letter was a vast relief, and very helpful too. And I am now *slowly* imagining my way back in to the book. The truth is that I seem to have got rather overtired, so I had to give up last week and am taking ten days off, eating yeast and vitamins and hoping to emerge like Popeye full of beans in a few days.

Meanwhile I have made a wholly new beginning with Hilary waking on the day of the interview, establishing her and also her relations with the Finnish boy whom I mentioned as the final epiphany—in the course of that morning we get a great deal more about her marriage. This should turn into about 60 pages and would be Part I. Part II might still be the interviewers on the way but with a major change in emphasis [, that is,] some tension between them which makes them active participants—and makes it possible for the interview later to act *on* them—this I see as fairly short, not more than 15 pages. I will then get to work at enriching what you saw and here all your criticism is most helpful. I have been pondering what you said about Hilary's seeming to be involved with people stronger than her . . . this suggests that there must be one more relationship I think—the Muse as antagonist.

I won't bother you with any more of this ruminating but I just wanted you to know that your letter fell on fallow ground. It gave me courage, too. I find this book the hardest I have ever conquered and I am now rather like a climber of Mt. Everest in camp somewhere below the summit, gazing up and wondering whether he will ever make it! Meanwhile the climb will certainly be interesting and I am very thankful that I had planned to take a full year off from teaching . . . that was the right decision, whatever the risks [ellipsis, Sarton's].

4 June 1964

Dear May,

I am just back as of yesterday and find your letter of May 25, which pleased me mightily. I am not pleased to hear that you had to go on vitamin pills, but the fact that you have got a new attack on Hilary is great.

Incidentally, your reference to climbing Mt. Everest is an entertaining association of ideas. It may not have been Sir Edmund Hilary who said it while conquering Everest, but some mountaineer said that the way to climb is to have a mental model of the entire mountain in mind, but while climbing you should never look at the summit, just keep putting one foot in front of the other. How the hell I am going to apply this to literary creation, I don't know. In fact I leave it at that.

2 September 1964

Dear May,
    I envy you that month in Belgium. I hope it has refreshed the cre-
ative spirit. It's good news that the novel seems to be taking a tighter
and better shape. Perhaps very annoyingly to you, I am delighted to
hear that it has seemed so hard and created so much anxiety in you. I
realize this is easy for me to say and hard for you to bear, but I suspect
the results may be your best. That is my feeling from what I have read
to date.
    Please let me know if there is anything I can do.


8 December 1964 [written from Yaddo]

Dear Eric,
    Diarmuid will have sent the book over to you. I am prepared for the
worst, but I do have one idea which I want you to think about as you
read it. Or, if you have read it, to think about now. What if we forgot
all about the term "novel" and invented some other word or phrase?—
I have not caught the right one but what I am after is something like
"A meditation on love and poetry in the form of a novel: or

                     The Interview
                Some Reporters and a Poet pursue
                     the Muse

                     The Interview:
                An Old Woman considers love and poetry

                     The Interview
                A [Literary] Fugue on Love and Poetry
                Fictional

    I have never imagined that this book would have huge numbers of
readers, you know. The problem has always been that it dealt in *essence*
as a poem rather than a novel usually does. *If* the whole concept of
what a novel is, or should be, is dropped out, then does not some thing
viable make itself known? This is Sarton's last stand!
    It's such a queer year, Eric—I have just heard that Wellesley can no
longer use me: the new curriculum precludes the teaching of poetry

writing. I didn't mean to mention this but it is, of course, much in my mind as to how to earn my living. But disaster can be a stimulus, and as I watch the juncos in the snow, how brave they are, I am ready for anything.

I might add that the Mss was read by a friend of mine who is writing a book on Henry James—a prof. of English at Agnes Scott [Ellen Dougles Leyburn]. She could not be torn away from it (much to my surprise) even to eat and read it through at one sitting. She felt it was a real achievement. Although she is personally interested of course, still the *degree* of her interest was encouraging.

Well—the defence [*sic*] rests.


9 December 1964

Dear May,

The manuscript has just arrived. Both Carol and I will read it as soon as possible (this is Directors' Meeting and sales conference time and so it may be a few days) and let you know. I am fascinated by your wish to approach it from a new angle rather than as a straight novel, but of course I cannot have an opinion until after I have read it.

I am distressed to hear about Wellesley's decision to drop your course. It cannot help but be a severe dislocation for you. I have absolutely no doubt, however, that you will meet the dislocation and turn it to use.

Until shortly,


12 January 1965

Dear May,

Both Carol Houck and I have read the novel—and I, unlike you, see no reason not to call it a novel. To my mind, it is superb, perhaps the best novel you have ever written. I have so few quibbles that I feel almost guilty at not exercising my franchise as an editor. However, I do have one or two queries to raise.

In the hospital scene, there is a brief suggestion that Hilary had been having the beginnings of an affair with the nurse. I wonder if this serves any purpose or whether it is one too many without much purpose. Hilary has a great many relationships; perhaps this one can go.

(I do see that it serves to point out that the doctor knows all of Hilary.)

Now to some nitpicking, and I am assuming that you have a carbon copy of the manuscript. [Omitted here are nineteen brief suggestions for specific changes in wording that require no substantive changes in the content. These suggestions are not easily understood out of context.]

You have completely solved all the problems I found in the first draft. Hilary is no longer the passive element in all her relationships. Peter is now completely acceptable, and your ideas are totally clear.

As I have said, I think this is a superb piece of work. I am convinced that it should be billed as a novel, and not as anything else. It is all the things that you suggest in your letter, but it is a novel, and if we suggest that it is not, I think it could cause you considerable anguish. As it is, I suspect I know something of the pain you suffered in writing this, and I think that it is one of the sources of its strength. I would be delinquent if I did not tell you that it will in any case be viewed as self-revaluation [sic; "revelation" probably intended], and I assume that you are prepared for the shock that will be felt by a good number of your readers. You may lose them. For us, and for many, what you have done, you have done with perception and purity.

We will get on to Diarmuid about terms. For now, congratulations.

19 January 1965

Dear May,

Many thanks for your wonderful letter of the 16th. It shows once again that you are one of the few authors who has a genuine wisdom about her own publishing problems as well as her writing problems.

I now entirely agree with you about the hospital scene. Don't change it. One thing that I still think needs improving is the title. Titles are a hideous problem. It seems to me that "The Interview" is neither very informative nor very pricking to the curiosity. I wish we could find something that does the same sort of job as "The Roman Spring of Mrs. Stone," or "The Middle Age of Mrs. Eliot." (Please don't think I am comparing these books to yours.) Another title which worked on the same problem was "The Left Hand is the Dreamer." We will all put ours [sic] minds to it and try to come up with some ideas, assuming that you are not fixed on this title.

I will pass your feelings about the book jacket on to our designers. As for the catalogue copy, which will then become the blurb on the jacket, I would very much like it if you would have a fling at it. If you don't want to do this, perhaps you would be willing simply to jot down some thoughts concerning the book—what it means and what should be emphasized in presenting it.

About Francis Brown of The Times: I should avoid writing him at all costs. The Times is as sensitive as a violet about what it thinks is an attempt to influence its reviewers. However, we can pass the word through other channels, in the hopes that it will reach him, and perhaps it will influence him. Could you by any chance see if you can remember the name of the woman who usually reviews your books? That would be a great help. [Sarton wrote at the bottom of Swenson's letter the name Elizabeth Janeway, who had reviewed *The Small Room* in the *New York Times Book Review* 20 August 1961.]

I am delighted to hear about the new book of verse. What is your schedule on it? Could it be ready for publication in the spring of 1966?


11 February 1965

Dear May,

MRS. STEVENS HEARS THE MERMAIDS SINGING is now the title. For some reason, between the time you first proposed it and now, we have fallen for it. It is a rare event when the sales department, editor, and author all agree on a title. Let's hope this is a good omen.

# Notes and References

*Chapter One*

1. Unless otherwise noted, all references to manuscript letters written by May Sarton and by George Sarton are made to their respective papers in the Henry W. and Albert A. Berg Collection, New York Public Library, Astor, Lenox, and Tilden Foundations. In all cases when a manuscript letter date is incomplete, I have used the date established for that letter by the Berg Collection.

2. May Sarton, *I Knew a Phoenix: Sketches for an Autobiography* (New York: W. W. Norton, 1959), 81; cited hereafter in parentheses in the text as *P* followed by page number.

3. Dr. Sarton brought *Isis* to America in 1915 and paid its annual deficits from then until 1940. *Isis* was begun as an international quarterly focusing on the history and philosophy of science. Dr. Sarton also began *Osiris,* a journal devoted to the history and philosophy of science and to the history of learning and culture.

4. *Letters to May,* with an introduction by May Sarton (Orono, Maine: Puckerbrush Press, 1986); cited hereafter in parentheses in the text as *LM* followed by page number.

5. Dr. Sarton had early learned Latin and Greek. As his scholarly life increased, his languages vastly expanded to include a reading knowledge of Arabic, Sanskrit, Chinese, Japanese, some other Asiatic languages as well as many of the languages of European countries. All three of the Sartons were fluent in French, but they always spoke English in their home.

6. These letters affected Sarton deeply. She wrote to her mother on 4 January 1936 and shows the distress her father's letters could cause. "Daddy wrote me a savage letter about two books which I shall hunt up in the next few days. I know now exactly where they are. But I am afraid of his power to hurt. The world seems such a senselessly cruel place that I hope at least I shall never be cruel like that" (Manuscript letter, 4 January 1936).

7. The obituary for George Sarton in the *New York Times* (23 March 1956, 27:1) noted that "virtually everything of a period occupied his attention, whether theology, art, linguistics, geography, politics, trade practices, crafts, social upheaval, or the technical procedures of ancient and medieval physicists and astronomers."

8. Carolyn G. Heilbrun, "May Sarton's Memoirs," in *May Sarton: Woman and Poet,* ed. Constance Hunting (Orono, Maine: National Poetry Foundation, 1982), 50.

9. Dr. Sarton had been named a research associate of the Carnegie Institute in Washington in 1918. Then in 1920, he joined the faculty at Harvard where he was made a full professor in 1940.

10. May Sarton was well-established in the Civic Repertory Theatre as an apprentice by 1920 when her father visited New York and sent his wife this telegram (8 May), a tangible sign that Eva Le Gallienne continued to support Sarton's career in the theater. "Had a good talk with Eva Le Gallienne yesternight. She believes May has a real vocation; advises us to encourage her. This afternoon witnessed marvelous performance of Romeo & Juliet. Shall be home tomorrow." When the Civic Repertory played Philadelphia, 7–21 April 1930, May Sarton was a page in *Romeo and Juliet*.

11. The Apprentice Theatre was serious about the theater. In 1932 Sarton spent six days conducting five hundred auditions for the company. In that same year the New School for Social Research engaged the Apprentice Theatre to produce ten European plays as one of its courses. From all accounts, it was a successful undertaking.

12. Sarton's theater life was rich and varied—she was actress, director, and for a time playwright. *Trelawney* was staged at Concord Academy in 1940; *The Underground River* was published in 1947. As late as 1953 Sarton still had playwriting on her mind. She wrote Louise Bogan that the light and charming work she was reading, *Good Morning, Miss Dove* by the North Carolinian Frances Gray Patton, interests Le Gallienne. She thought Miss Dove would be a perfect role for her. "I might," Sarton wrote, "try my hand at a dramatization" (Manuscript letter, 6 January 1955, Amherst College Library). Another project Sarton considered at this time was turning *A Shower of Summer Days* into a drama, if the *Good Morning, Miss Dove* did not work out. She finished neither project. While playwriting does continue to interest Sarton, a return to acting never did.

13. Heilbrun, "Sarton's Memoirs," 45.

14. A French rendering does perhaps "sound" more sense than does the English—"Mes roses—mes roses sont tres jolie. Elles se fondent dans l'air"— but the response to Mansfield's words may simply be the enthusiasm of a first reading.

15. *What the Woman Lived: Selected Letters of Louise Bogan, 1920–1970,* edited and with an introduction by Ruth Limmer (New York: Harcourt Brace Jovanovich, 1973).

16. Manuscript letter (21 April 1940), May Sarton to Louise Bogan, Amherst College Library.

17. Manuscript letter (24 April 1940), Louise Bogan to May Sarton, Berg Collection.

18. Manuscript letter (15 August 1954), May Sarton to Louise Bogan, Amherst College Library.

19. Manuscript letter (13 November 1953), May Sarton to Louise Bogan, Amherst College Library.

20. Manuscript letter (4 January 1954), Louise Bogan to May Sarton, Berg Collection.
21. Elizabeth Frank, *Louise Bogan. A Portrait* (New York: Knopf, 1985).
22. May Sarton, *Journal of Solitude* (New York: W. W. Norton, 1973), 130; cited hereafter in parentheses in the text as *JS* followed by page number.
23. Frank, *Bogan,* 353.
24. Ibid., 357.
25. Manuscript letter (13 March 1954), Louise Bogan to May Sarton, Berg Collection.
26. Manuscript letter (10 March 1950) May Sarton to Louise Bogan, Amherst College Library.
27. Manuscript letter (1953), William Theo Brown to May Sarton, Berg Collection.
28. May Sarton, *A World of Light: Portraits and Celebrations* (New York: W. W. Norton, 1976), 242; hereafter cited in parentheses in the text as *WL* followed by page number.
29. *The Letters of Virginia Woolf, 1936–1941,* ed. Nigel Nicholson and Joanne Trautmann (New York: Harcourt Brace Jovanovich, 1980): 6:314, 165, 181.

*Chapter Two*

1. Frank, "Approaches to Autobiography," in *May Sarton: Woman and Poet,* 33.
2. Suzanne Owens, "House, Home and Solitude," in *May Sarton: Woman and Poet,* 58.
3. Heilbrun, "Sarton's Memoirs," 44.
4. Sarton recounts her version of the "Miss Lovelace episode" when she writes her portrait of Elizabeth Bowen in *A World of Light* (109). Victoria Glendenning gives her version in *Elizabeth Bowen* (New York: Avon Books, 1979), 220–21.
5. Heilbrun, "Sarton's Memoirs," 43.
6. Ibid., 46, 48.
7. *Recovering* (New York: W. W. Norton, 1980), 9; cited hereafter in the text as *R* followed by page number.
8. *The House by the Sea* (New York: W. W. Norton, 1977), 28; cited hereafter in the text as *HS* followed by page number.
9. *At Seventy* (New York: W. W. Norton, 1984), 183; cited hereafter in the text as *S* followed by page number.
10. *Plant Dreaming Deep* (New York: W. W. Norton, 1968), 15; cited hereafter in parentheses in the text as *PD* followed by page number.
11. Richard Rhodes, "How the Summer People Learned to Pass the Winter," review of *Kinds of Love, New York Times Book Review,* 29 November 1970, 56.

12. *After the Stroke* (New York: W. W. Norton, 1988), 279.

13. Nancy Mairs, "Taking a Leap into Old Age," review of *After the Stroke, New York Times Book Review,* 27 March 1988, 30.

*Chapter Three*

1. *The Complete Poems of Emily Dickinson,* ed. Thomas H. Johnson (Boston: Little, Brown & Co., 1960) 399.

2. Gayle Gaskill, "Redefinitions of Traditional Christian Emblems and Outlooks in May Sarton's Novels of 1970–1975," in *May Sarton: Woman and Poet,* 163, 167, 169.

3. *The Bridge of Years* (New York: Doubleday, 1946), 26; hereafter pages cited in parentheses in the text. Sarton wrote William Theo Brown (14 September 1945) that the title of this novel was "In Parenthesis"; however, Doubleday did not like it. *The Bridge of Years,* she wrote Brown, is the best she can come up with—"a quiet statement of the fact. But not perhaps too exciting."

4. *A Shower of Summer Days,* (New York: Rinehart, 1957), 151; pages cited hereafter in parentheses in the text.

5. *The Birth of a Grandfather* (New York: Rinehart, 1957), 43; pages cited hereafter in parentheses in the text.

6. *Kinds of Love* (New York: W. W. Norton, 1970), 17; pages cited hereafter in parentheses in the text.

7. Margaret Atwood, "That Certain Thing Called the Girlfriend," *New York Times Book Review,* 11 May 1986, 39. Jane S. Bakerman, in a 1978 article, looked at love and friendships between women in *The Birth of a Grandfather, A Small Room, Mrs. Stevens Hears the Mermaids Singing, Kinds of Love,* and *As We Are Now.* She anticipates Atwood's point when she says, "Sarton is one of the very few writers to present a vivid picture of the importance and the nourishment of friendship between women" (*"Kinds of Love:* Love and Friendship in Novels of May Sarton," *Critique* 20 [1978]: 90).

8. *Crucial Conversations* (New York: W. W. Norton, 1975), 35.

9. *Anger* (New York: W. W. Norton, 1982), 84; pages cited hereafter in parentheses in the text.

10. *Faithful Are the Wounds* (New York: Rinehart, 1955; reprint, W. W. Norton, 1972), 5; pages cited hereafter in parentheses in the text.

11. *The Single Hound* (Boston: Houghton Mifflin, 1938), 55; pages cited hereafter in parentheses in the text.

12. *Mrs. Stevens Hears the Mermaids Singing,* with an introduction by Carolyn G. Heilbrun (New York: W. W. Norton, 1974), xv; pages cited hereafter in parentheses in the text. On 24 June 1965 Sarton wrote Basil de Selincourt an interesting passage about herself, her self-revelation, and *Mrs. Stevens:* "And I have waited until I had a firm reputation and had written enough books which show that I understand and am *for* the normal human

situation, so that this should take its place in the series of novels as one out of nine or ten. I felt it would be dishonest not to come out into the open—that this was mandatory for my own true relation with *myself*. And now it is done, I doubt the subject will come up again in any future work. The new book of poems, by the way, has no love poems in it, and this also is deliberate" (Berg Collection, New York Public Library).

13. Carolyn G. Heilbrun, *Reinventing Womanhood* (New York: W. W. Norton, 1979), 89.

14. Virginia Woolf, *To the Lighthouse* (1927; reprint, New York: Harcourt, Brace, 1955), 48.

15. *The Magnificent Spinster* (New York: W. W. Norton, 1985), 269; pages cited hereafter in parentheses in the text.

16. *As We Are Now* (New York: W. W. Norton, 1973), 81.

17. *A Reckoning* (New York: W. W. Norton, 1981), 190; pages cited hereafter in parentheses in the text.

18. Carolyn G. Heilbrun, *Toward a Recognition of Androgyny* (New York: W. W. Norton, 1982), 28.

19. See Bakerman, *"Kinds of Love:* Love and Friendship in Novels of May Sarton."

20. The setting of the novel (as Sarton points out in *A World of Light*) is a great house in Ireland, Dene's Court, a thinly disguised picture of Bowen's Court where Sarton had visited with her friend, the novelist Elizabeth Bowen. Sarton's impressions give her fictional house features of Elizabeth Bowen's ancestral home. For example, Violet explains that the flight of stairs that should lead to the ballroom are missing "because the money ran out." Victoria Glendenning, Bowen's biographer, reports this same circumstance at Bowen's Court: "The staircase, lighted by Venetian window had oak banisters and opened on to a gallery on the second floor; from here the stairs were to have extended upwards, but no Bowen had ever had the money to do it; as it was, the Long Room could only be reached by humble backstairs" (Glendenning, *Elizabeth Bowen,* 79). And like Elizabeth Bowen, Violet hated moths.

21. *The Small Room* (New York: W. W. Norton, 1961), 17, 19. *The Small Room* interested reviewers particularly as a "college novel." Elizabeth Janeway reviewed it for the *New York Times Book Review* (20 August 1961) and praised what she called "a serious novel about the serious work of a college" (5).

22. Heilbrun, *Androgyny,* 13.

23. Irene Claremont de Castillejo, *Knowing Woman: Feminine Psychology* (New York: Harper & Row, 1974), 15.

24. Heilbrun, *Androgyny,* 142.

25. Doris Grumbach, review of *Crucial Conversations, New York Times Book Review,* 27 April 1975, 4.

26. John Gardner, review of *Mrs. Stevens Hears the Mermaids Singing, Southern Review* 3 (Spring 1967):455.

27. Louise Bogan, "The Eight-Sided Heart," Watershed Tapes, Archive Series, no. C-159, 1984.

28. *The Poet and the Donkey* (New York: W. W. Norton, 1969), 145; pages cited hereafter in parentheses in the text.

29. *Joanna and Ulysses* (New York: W. W. Norton, 1963), 13; pages cited hereafter in parentheses in the text. Sarton wrote Basil de Selincourt on 30 April 1963 that *Joanna and Ulysses* "may now be made into a movie! I get $1000 on an option and if they do it, another 9 thousand. So I shall have a second chance to *save*—maybe! What a miracle." On 14 January 1965 she reported that "the movie people have extended the option of J. and U. for another three months—so they are seriously trying to raise money to do the film, and they are the producers of a [very] sensitive film called David and Lisa so I would like them to do it" (Berg Collection, New York Public Library). As is often the case of novels that receive an option, *Joanna and Ulysses* has not been made into a movie.

30. *The Fur Person* (New York: Rinehart, 1957; reprint, W. W. Norton, 1968), 7; pages cited in parentheses hereafter in the text.

31. *Shadow of a Man* (New York: Rinehart, 1950), 25; pages cited in parentheses hereafter in the text.

*Chapter Four*

1. Manuscript letter (12 October 1955), Amherst College Library.

2. *Selected Poems of May Sarton,* edited and with an introduction by Serena Sue Hilsinger and Lois Brynes (New York: W. W. Norton, 1978), 9; cited hereafter in the text.

3. *A Private Mythology* (New York: W. W. Norton, 1966), 79; cited hereafter in the text.

4. Alicia Ostriker, *Stealing the Language: The Emergence of Women's Poetry in America* (Boston: Beacon Press, 1986), 7–8.

5. Sarton's poem, "The Tortured," in *The Lion and the Rose,* 1948, uses the abstractions of innocence and wisdom as well as the familial relationships of the mother and child to voice the horror of the Nazi camps, the unspeakable suffering that transpired. Her essay "Revision as Creation" provides the germ of this poem—the story of a gentle Belgian cousin, the weakling of the family, "who, when the supreme test came of withstanding torture and not telling, found it in him to die rather than to speak" (*Writings on Writing* [Orono, Maine: Puckerbrush Press, 1980], 64; cited hereafter in the text as *WW* followed by page number).

6. Eudora Welty, *The Eye of the Story: Selected Essays and Reviews* (New York: Random House, 1977), 148.

7. Letters from Basil de Selincourt to May Sarton are part of the May Sarton Papers, Berg Collection, New York Public Library, from which quotations follow.

8. *In Time Like Air* (New York: Rinehart, 1958), 49.

9. *The Lion and the Rose* (New York: Rinehart, 1948), 15; pages cited hereafter parenthetically in the text.

10. The South, however, has continued to raise Sarton's ire when she encounters Southerners who display pretentious manners along with insensitivity to race relations. On occasion, her liberal views have clashed with those of conservative Southern hosts. Journal entries take up this point from time to time.

11. Berg Collection, New York Public Library.

12. Constance Hunting, "The Risk Is Very Great," in *May Sarton: Woman and Poet,* 203, 206.

13. Sandra M. Gilbert and Susan Gubar, eds., *Norton Anthology of Literature by Women: The Tradition in English* (New York: W. W. Norton, 1985). Gilbert and Gubar include "My Sisters, O My Sisters," "Letter from Chicago. For Virginia Woolf," and "The Muse as Medusa."

14. *A Durable Fire* (New York: W. W. Norton, 1972), 66; pages cited hereafter in parentheses in the text.

15. *A Grain of Mustard Seed* (New York: W. W. Norton, 1971), 57–58.

16. *Cloud, Stone, Sun, Vine* (New York: W. W. Norton, 1961), 140–41.

17. Maureen Connelly has examined five of Sarton's garden poems in "Metaphor in Five Garden Poems by May Sarton," in *May Sarton: Woman and Poet,* 187–92.

18. Henry Taylor, "The Singing Wound: Intensifying Paradoxes in May Sarton's 'A Divorce of Lovers,'" in *May Sarton: Woman and Poet,* 193–200.

19. Ibid., 193.

20. In her essay, "May Sarton's Memoirs," Carolyn Heilbrun emphasizes the contribution that *Plant Dreaming Deep* made to the literature about women: "What makes *Plant Dreaming Deep* unique and uniquely important, is that Sarton has written a memoir of the possibilities of the solitary female life, but without negatively defining the condition of those who are *just* women" (*May Sarton: Woman and Poet,* 46). Sarton's "women's poems" also positively portray independent women.

21. Ostriker, *Stealing the Language,* 215.

22. *Halfway to Silence* (New York: W. W. Norton, 1980), 48.

23. William Drake, *The First Wave: Women and Poets in America, 1915–1945* (New York: MacMillan, 1987). 261. Drake's excellent study focuses on that generation of women poets who came just before Sarton, but he places Sarton and Louise Bogan as harbingers of the new generation of poets.

24. Ibid., 261.

*Chapter Five*

1. George Sarton wrote to his daughter on 23 October 1932 admonishing her to remember "to thank Mevious Macleod for the 'Flemish heart'

she so thoughtfully gave you. Maybe she wanted you to remember that you
are a Flemish girl" (Manuscript letter, 23 October 1932).

2. Elaine Showalter, "Feminist Criticism in the Wilderness," in *Writing and Sexual Difference,*" ed. Elizabeth Abel (Chicago: University of Chicago Press, 1982), 35.

3. Ibid., 15.

4. See Nina Auerbach, "Magi and Maidens: The Romance of the Victorian Freud," in *Writing and Sexual Difference,* 111–30.

5. Deborah Pope, *A Separate Vision: Isolation in Contemporary Women's Poetry* (Baton Rouge: Louisiana State University Press, 1984), 50.

6. In the *New York Times Book Review* (24 December 1961, 5) Karl Shapiro reviewed three books of poetry: Isabella Gardner's *The Looking Glass,* which he praised extravagantly; Dilys Laing's posthumous *Poems from a Cage,* which he also praised; and May Sarton's *Cloud, Stone, Sun, Vine,* which he damned. The paragraph that he devotes to Sarton gives a needed context for the 1966 letter to Bogan. Sarton's sense of failure comes in part from Shapiro's unreasonably harsh attack:

It is pointless to be cruel about bad poetry, but sometimes there is no escape. Whatever May Sarton's other accomplishments as a writer, she is a bad poet. The present collection covers a twenty-year period of writing and none of it is distinguished in any way. Her poetry is lady-poetry at its worst—this at a time when poetry is very much the art of women. Her poems are personal in the sense that the reader is invited to participate in the higher life, as tourists visit the house of the Duke of Bedford. But the tour turns out to be a walk through the chamber of clichés; her high literary attitudes (Rilke and Yeats) are often hastily mastered techniques gaily applied for the occasion—I am sorry to say this. I apologize.

Two weeks later, 21 January 1972, the *Times* published short excerpts from letters protesting Shapiro's review. One was from Sarton's close friend, Judith Matlack, and one was from her old friend, the English critic Basil de Selincourt. The other three were from fans of May Sarton who wrote their protest and registered their complaint and outrage.

# Selected Bibliography

## PRIMARY WORKS

*Poetry*

### COLLECTIONS

*Collected Poems, 1930–1973.* New York: W. W. Norton, 1974.
*Selected Poems of May Sarton.* Edited by Serena Sue Hilsinger and Lois Brynes. New York: W. W. Norton, 1978.

### INDIVIDUAL VOLUMES

*As Does New Hampshire.* Concord, N.H.: Richard R. Smith, Publisher, 1967.
*Cloud, Stone, Sun, Vine: Poems Selected and New.* New York: W. W. Norton, 1961.
*A Durable Fire.* New York: W. W. Norton, 1972.
*Encounter in April.* Boston: Houghton Mifflin, 1937.
*A Grain of Mustard Seed.* New York: W. W. Norton, 1971.
*Halfway to Silence: New Poems.* New York: W. W. Norton, 1980.
*In Time Like Air.* New York: Rinehart, 1958.
*Inner Landscape.* Boston: Houghton Mifflin, 1939.
*Land of Silence and Other Poems.* New York: Rinehart, 1953.
*The Leaves of the Tree.* Mount Vernon, Iowa: Cornell College Chapbooks, 1950.
*Letters from Maine: New Poems.* New York: W. W. Norton, 1984.
*The Lion and the Rose.* New York: Rinehart, 1948.
*The Phoenix Again, New Poems.* Concord, N.H.: William B. Ewert, Publisher, 1987.
*A Private Mythology.* New York: W. W. Norton, 1966.
*The Silence Now: New and Uncollected Earlier Poems.* New York: W. W. Norton, 1988.

*Novels*

*Anger.* New York: W. W. Norton, 1982.
*As We Are Now.* New York: W. W. Norton, 1973.
*The Birth of a Grandfather.* New York: Rinehart, 1957.
*The Bridge of Years.* New York: Doubleday, 1946. Reprint, New York: W. W. Norton, 1979.
*Crucial Conversations.* New York: W. W. Norton, 1975.
*Faithful Are the Wounds.* New York: Rinehart, 1955. Reprint, New York: W. W. Norton, 1972.

*Kinds of Love.* New York: W. W. Norton, 1970. Reprint, A Reader's Digest Association Condensed Version, with biographical sketch, 1971.
*The Magnificent Spinster.* New York: W. W. Norton, 1985.
*Mrs. Stevens Hears the Mermaids Singing.* New York: W. W. Norton, 1965. Reprint with an introduction by Carolyn G. Heilbrun, New York: W. W. Norton, 1974.
*A Reckoning.* New York: W. W. Norton, 1981.
*Shadow of a Man.* New York: Rinehart, 1950.
*A Shower of Summer Days.* New York: Rinehart, 1952. Reprint, New York: W. W. Norton, 1970.
*The Single Hound.* Boston: Houghton Mifflin, 1938.
*The Small Room.* New York: W. W. Norton, 1961.

*Tales and Fables*

*The Fur Person.* New York: Rinehart, 1957. Reprint, New York: W. W. Norton, 1978.
*Joanna and Ulysses.* New York: W. W. Norton, 1963.
*Miss Pickthorne and Mr. Hare,* New York: W. W. Norton, 1966.
*The Poet and the Donkey.* New York: W. W. Norton, 1969.

*Children's Books*

*Punch's Secret.* New York: Harper & Row, 1974.
*A Walk through the Woods.* New York: Harper & Row, 1976.

*Criticism and Letters*

*Letters to May,* with an introduction by May Sarton. Orono, Maine: Puckerbrush Press, 1986.
*Writings on Writing.* Orono, Maine: Puckerbrush Press, 1980.

*Memoirs and Journals*

*After the Stroke.* New York: W. W. Norton, 1988.
*At Seventy.* New York: W. W. Norton, 1984.
*Honey in the Hive: Judith Matlack 1898–1982.* Boston: Warren Publishing, 1988.
*The House by the Sea.* New York: W. W. Norton, 1977.
*I Knew a Phoenix: Sketches for an Autobiography.* New York: Holt, Rinehart & Winston, 1959. Reprint, New York: W. W. Norton, 1969.
*Journal of a Solitude.* New York: W. W. Norton, 1973.
*Plant Dreaming Deep.* New York: W. W. Norton, 1968.
*Recovering.* New York: W. W. Norton, 1980.
*A World of Light: Portraits and Celebrations.* New York: W. W. Norton, 1976.

*Recordings*

*May Sarton: A Self-Portrait.* Edited by Marita Simpson and Martha Wheelock. New York: W. W. Norton, 1982. Transcription of the film, *World of Light: A Portrait of May Sarton.*

May Sarton. "My Sisters, O My Sisters." Watershed Tapes, Signature Series. No. CO170. Washington, D.C.: The Watershed Foundation, 1984.

May Sarton. "Interview" and "May Sarton reads excerpts from *As We Are Now* and *Journal of a Solitude.*" Columbia, Mo.: American Audio Prose Library, 1982.


SECONDARY WORKS

*Bibliography*

Blouin, Lenora P. *May Sarton: A Bibliography.* Scarecrow Author Bibliography, no. 34. Metuchen, N.J.: Scarecrow Press, 1978. Blouin published "A Revised Bibliography" in *May Sarton: Woman and Poet,* 283–322. Orono, Maine: National Poetry Foundation, 1982.

*Books*

Hunting, Constance, ed. *May Sarton: Woman and Poet.* Orono, Maine: National Poetry Foundation, 1982. Twenty-four essays on Sarton's memoirs, journals, novels, and poetry comprise this useful book. Especially important are Carolyn Heilbrun's careful separation of "memoir" and "journal" and Mary Lydon's "A French View of May Sarton," which furnishes the best study to date on the influence of French prose style on Sarton. In this book Lenora Blouin updates her Sarton bibliography with primary titles listed and with annotated reviews from 1978 to 1981.

Sibly, Agnes. *May Sarton.* New York: Twayne Publishers, 1972. A discussion and evaluation of Sarton's primary work through 1972.

*Articles and Parts of Books*

Anderson, Dawn Holt. "May Sarton's Women." In *Images of Women in Fiction,* edited by Susan K. Cornillon, 243–50. Bowling Green, Ohio: Bowling Green University Popular Press, 1972. Using three Sarton novels, Anderson emphasizes Sarton's success in providing models for women who acknowledge and embrace solitude and who insist on finding and claiming their own identity.

Atwood, Margaret. "That Certain Thing Called the Girlfriend." *New York Times Book Review,* 11 May 1986, 39. Atwood claims the friendship of women as subject matter for serious fiction.

Bakerman, Jane S. "*Kinds of Love:* Love and Friendship in Novels of May
    Sarton." *Critique* 20 (1978): 83–91. Focusing on five of Sarton's novels,
    Bakerman suggests that Sarton's most sensitive and mature characters
    must "'create' themselves in order to really be." Bakerman places Sarton
    as "one of the very few American writers to present a vivid picture of the
    importance and the nourishment of friendship between women."
Bernikow, Louise. *Among Women.* New York: Harper, 1980. Although not
    drawing directly from Sarton, Bernikow's useful book discusses "what
    actually happens in women's lives" and the literary accounts of many
    relationships between women.
Bowles, Gloria. *Louise Bogan's Aesthetics of Limitation.* Bloomington: Indiana
    University Press, 1987. Shows May Sarton's perceptive understanding of
    Bogan's struggle to balance her life as poetry critic and her impulse to be
    a poet.
Drake, William. *The First Wave: Women and Poets in America, 1915–1945.*
    New York: MacMillan, 1987. Traces the lives and public reputations of
    twenty-seven well-known and little-known women poets who published
    between 1915 and 1945. Sarton is treated in the concluding chapter as a
    harbinger of a new generation of poets.
Frank, Elizabeth P. *Louise Bogan: A Portrait.* New York: Knopf, 1985. Thor-
    oughly analyzes the personal and professional friendship of May Sarton
    and Louise Bogan.
Glendenning, Victoria. *Elizabeth Bowen.* New York: Avon Books, 1979. Dis-
    cusses the friendship of Elizabeth Bowen and May Sarton.
Heilbrun, Carolyn G. *Reinventing Womanhood.* New York: W. W. Norton,
    1979. In this forceful study Heilbrun argues that women must not for-
    sake "the imagination of wholeness" either in their own ambition or in
    their literature. Womanhood, thus, must be reinvented and female ex-
    perience must not be dominated or monopolized by men.
———. *Toward a Recognition of Androgyny.* New York: W. W. Norton, 1982.
    Heilbrun argues against "sexual polarization" and "the prison of gender"
    and urges readers to freely choose modes of behavior. The ideal mode, she
    argues, is the state of androgyny.
Limmer, Ruth, ed. *What the Woman Lived: Selected Letters of Louise Bogan,
    1920–1970.* New York: Harcourt Brace Jovanovich, 1973. Contains let-
    ters from Louise Bogan to May Sarton, but few letters are published
    entire.
Nicholson, Nigel, and Joanne Trautmann, ed. *The Letters of Virginia Woolf,
    1936–1941.* New York: Harcourt Brace Jovanovich, 1980. Contains let-
    ters to May Sarton and references about her in letters to various
    correspondents.
Ostriker, Alicia. *Stealing the Language: The Emergence of Women's Poetry in Amer-
    ica.* Boston: Beacon Press, 1986. In a first-rate appraisal of women's po-

etry, Ostriker explores the sources, context, and the meaning of
contemporary American women poets. She examines poems in form,
style, and especially language to trace the emerging voice of women poets
and considers Sarton particularly as a poet who treats women's relationship to myth.

Rule, Jane. "May Sarton." In *Lesbian Images*. New York: Doubleday, 1979. In
a chapter on Sarton, Rule discusses Sarton's position as novelist, focusing
her analysis on *Mrs. Stevens Hears the Mermaids Singing*.

Tomalin, Claire. *Katherine Mansfield: A Secret Life*. London: Viking, 1987.
Useful not only because of Sarton's early devotion to Mansfield but also
for the interesting portrayal of Sarton's devoted friend, Soloman Solo-
monovich Koteliansky (1882–1955).

# Index

Aiken, Conrad, 20
Atwood, Margaret, 48
Auden, Wystan Hugh, 15

Bachelard, Gaston, 83
Beach, Sylvia, 20
Bishop, Elizabeth, 14, 79
Bloomsbury, 38
Bogan, Louise, 13–18, 25, 65, 68, 77,
  92–93, 106, 111–12, 114–15,
  128n12; letters, 14; *Poems and New
  Poems,* 15; poetry critic, *New Yorker,*
  14, 17, 77, 111–12; marriages, 16;
  poems: "Daemon, The," 111; "Furies,
  The," 111; "Psychiatrist's Song,"
  111; "Kept," 111, "Evening in the
  Sanitarium," 114–15; "M., Singing,"
  16
Bowen, Elizabeth, 20, 22, 25, 27, 107,
  116–17, 129n4, 131n20
Brown, William Theo, 18–19, 20, 22,
  78, 82, 94

Cabot, Richard C., 10
Cather, Willa, 37; *My Ántonia,* 43–44
Chekhov, Anton: *Cherry Orchard, The,* 9;
  *Seagull, The,* 8
Cheever, John, 32
Chopin, Kate, 43, 48
Closset, Marie (Jean Dominique), 6, 20,
  25, 55
Coles, Robert: *Children in Crisis,* 80

de Castillejo, Irene Claremont: *Knowing
  Women: A Feminine Psychology,* 62
de Selincourt, Basil, 81, 88, 116,
  130n12, 134n6
Dickinson, Emily, 8, 42, 105
Dineson, Isak: *Out of Africa,* 117
Drake, William, 111, 112
Duse, Eleanor, 107

Eliot, Thomas Stearns: "Boston Evening
  Transcript, The," 74; "Love Song of
  J. Alfred Prufrock, The," 64

Flanner, Janet, 20
Frank, Elizabeth: *Louise Bogan: A
  Portrait,* 16, 111

Gaskill, Gayle, 43

Hall, Volta (psychiatrist), 92, 93
Heilbrun, Carolyn G., 4, 11, 25–26,
  57, 62, 63, 64; Introduction to *Mrs.
  Stevens Hears the Mermaids Singing,* 52,
  63, 64; *Reinventing Womanhood,* 63;
  *Toward a Recognition of Androgyny,* 57,
  62
H. D. (Hilda Doolittle), 20, 21
Hindemith, Paul, 19
Huxley, Julian and Juliette, 21, 25

"I'm Too Busy To Talk Now: Interviews
  with Artists over Seventy" (PBS radio
  interview), 97
Ibsen, Henrik: *Master Builder, The,* 10,
  11

Koteliansky, S. S. (Kot), 20, 25, 82, 94

Lawrence, D. H., 20
Le Gallienne, Eva, 7, 8, 9, 10, 25,
  128n12; Civic Repertory Theater, 7,
  10, 25, 128n10
Limbosch family, 76, 97; Raymond, 14
Lugne-Poe, 25, 91

Mansfield, Katherine, 12–13, 20, 94
Matisse, 83
Matlack, Judith, 20, 40, 72, 92, 93,
  94, 134n6
Moore, Marianne, 20, 22

140

Nabokov, Vladimir and Vera, 72
Nazimova, Alla, 9
*Norton Anthology of Literature by Women*,
92, 108

O'Connor, Flannery: "Artificial Nigger,
The," 28
O'Keeffe, Georgia, 107
Ostriker, Alicia, 79, 110

Pitter, Ruth, 14, 15, 19–20, 21
Poulenc, Francis, 19

Rukeyser, Muriel, 20, 22, 79, 88
Russell, Diarmuid, 118, 119, 122, 124

Sackville-West, Vita, 94–95
Sarton, Arthur (great-uncle), 97

Sarton, Eléanor Marie (May): androgyny,
58–63; early reading habits, 11–13;
education, 5–7; European ties, 1–2,
23, 74, 76, 84, 97, 113, 117; first
publications, 13; friendship between
women, 37, 47–48, 130n7;
homosexuality, 37, 60, 61, 62, 68–
69, 114, 130n12; interest in art, 2,
18; journal characteristics, 26–36,
39, 40–41; memoir characteristics,
24–26; the muse, 32, 33–34, 64–67,
70–71, 121; music, 16, 18–19, 23,
28; old age, 30, 35–36, 37, 39, 43,
48, 55–58, 69–70, 91–92; political
views, 40, 79–80, 81; relation with
father, 4–5, 96, 127n6; relation with
mother, 3–4, 94–96; solitude, 3, 26,
35, 38–39, 43; theater years, 7–11,
128n10; views on marriage, 44–55,
114; World War II, 19–20, 22, 40,
46, 72, 80; writers admired, 14, 41

WORKS—ESSAYS
*Writings on Writing* (book), 82
"Revision as Creation," 83
"School of Babylon, The," 81, 83
"Writing of a Poem, The," 83

WORKS—FABLES
*Fur Person, The*, 70, 72–73
*Joanna and Ulysses*, 48, 70, 71–72,
132n29
*Miss Pickthorne and Mr. Hare*, 70
*Poet and the Donkey, The*, 32, 70, 71

WORKS—FILM
*May Sarton: A World of Light* (film),
103, 108

WORKS—JOURNALS
*After the Stroke*, 26, 29, 35, 36, 40;
review by Nancy Mairs, 36
*At Seventy*, 9, 26, 27, 29, 31, 34, 35,
37, 39, 40, 72, 97
*House by the Sea, The*, 26, 27, 28, 29,
31, 34, 37, 39, 113
*Journal of a Solitude*, 16, 26, 31, 34,
37, 38, 39, 41
*Recovering*, 26, 29, 32, 33, 34, 35,
37, 39, 40, 41

WORKS—MEMOIRS
*Honey in the Hive* (includes poems by
Judith Matlack), 94
*I Knew a Phoenix*, 1, 2, 5, 7, 24, 25,
38
*Plant Dreaming Deep*, 24, 25, 26, 30,
31, 38, 113, 133n20
*World of Light, A*, 1, 2, 20, 24, 25,
31, 32, 95

WORKS—NOVELS
*Anger*, 32, 46, 49, 51–53, 57, 59
*As We Are Now*, 32, 33, 43, 48, 56
*Birth of a Grandfather, The*, 47, 50–
51, 55
*Bridge of Years, The*, 44–46, 47, 59
*Crucial Conversations*, 43, 48, 50;
review by Doris Grumbach, 63
*Faithful Are the Wounds*, 33, 49–50,
55
*Kinds of Love*, 31, 32, 36, 43, 45, 48,
50, 54, 55, 58; review by Richard
Rhodes, 31
*Magnificent Spinster, The*, 6, 42, 54,
59